AF348507

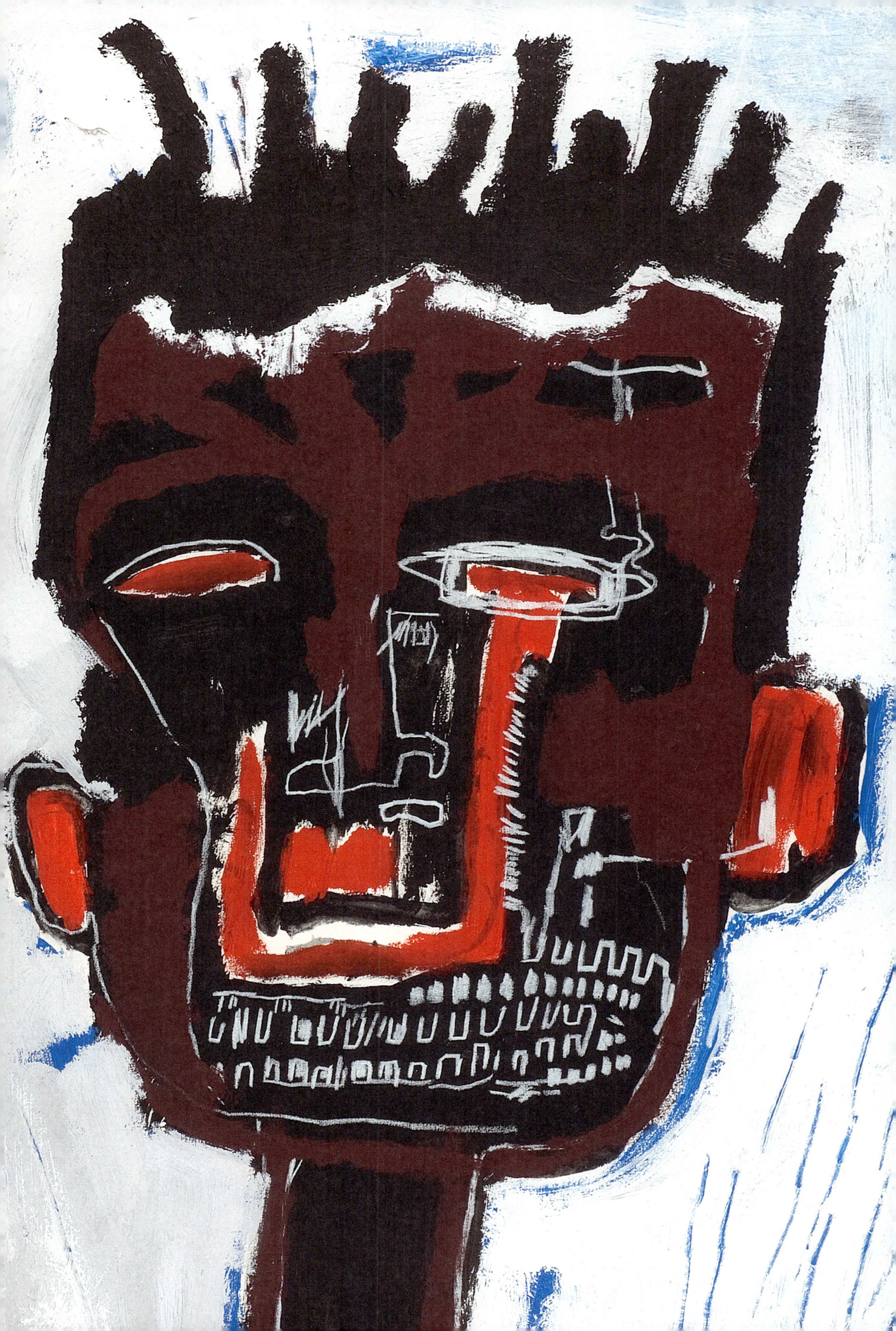

Jean-Michel Basquiat
Engadin

Hauser & Wirth Publishers

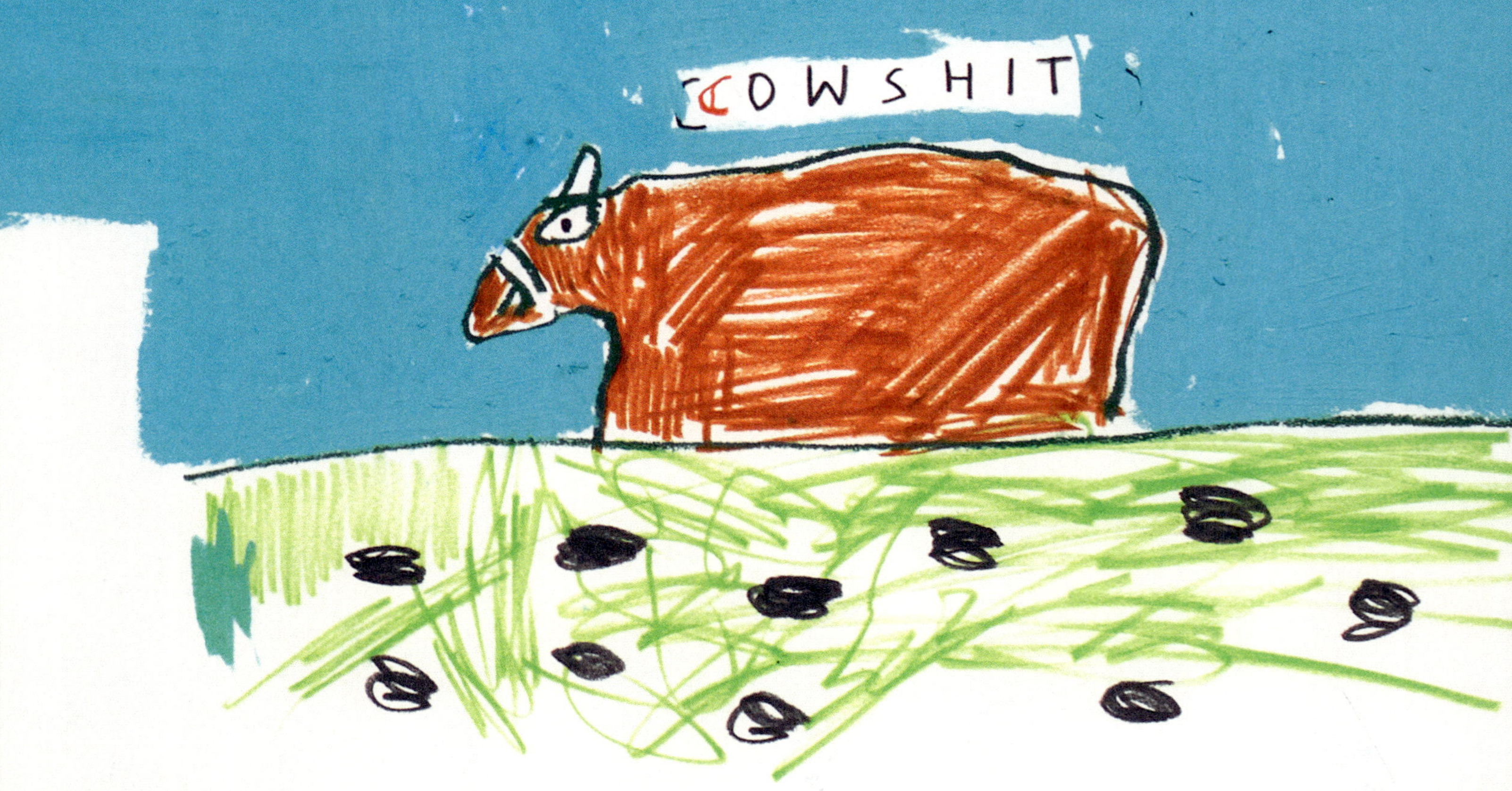

COWSHIT
BRATWURST

Foreword
Iwan Wirth

Bruno Bischofberger's proximity to the exceptional artists he represented has always been a great inspiration to me, and the anecdotes of his adventures with Jean-Michel Basquiat—such as their legendary visit to the Toggenburg bull show—are among my favorite descriptions of artist travels. The works created during Jean-Michel's stays with Bruno in St. Moritz capture the artist's impressions of the landscape and culture of the Swiss Alps in an incredible, energetic, and captivating manner. His time in Switzerland continued to echo even after the artist's return to the US, where works he made in New York include references to the famous bratwursts, for example, and German phrases.

Bringing together works created by Jean-Michel Basquiat both in and about Switzerland, *Jean-Michel Basquiat: Engadin* is the first survey exhibition and catalogue to reveal the artist's close connection to this Alpine country. Basquiat's link to Switzerland began with his first show at Galerie Bruno Bischofberger in Zurich in 1982, and it continued until 1986, encompassing several visits to St. Moritz, Zurich, and Appenzell together with Bischofberger. Our current undertaking pays homage not only to the trailblazing group of works that Basquiat created during these years but also to the unique and visionary relationship between the artist and his gallerist.

We are honored to present this extraordinary exhibition of highly personal works by one of the most important artists of the twentieth century at our gallery in St. Moritz. I am touched to see many of these works return to their place of origin.

Jean-Michel Basquiat: Engadin would not have been possible without Dieter Buchhart and Anna Karina Hofbauer, internationally renowned Basquiat experts who have shared their knowledge and provided invaluable assistance. My gratitude goes to Bruno and Yoyo Bischofberger and to the many lenders whose trust and generosity have helped bring this survey exhibition to life. I would also like to thank Nora Fitzpatrick, Lisane Basquiat, and Jeanine Heriveaux from the Estate of Jean-Michel Basquiat for their support of this ambitious project.

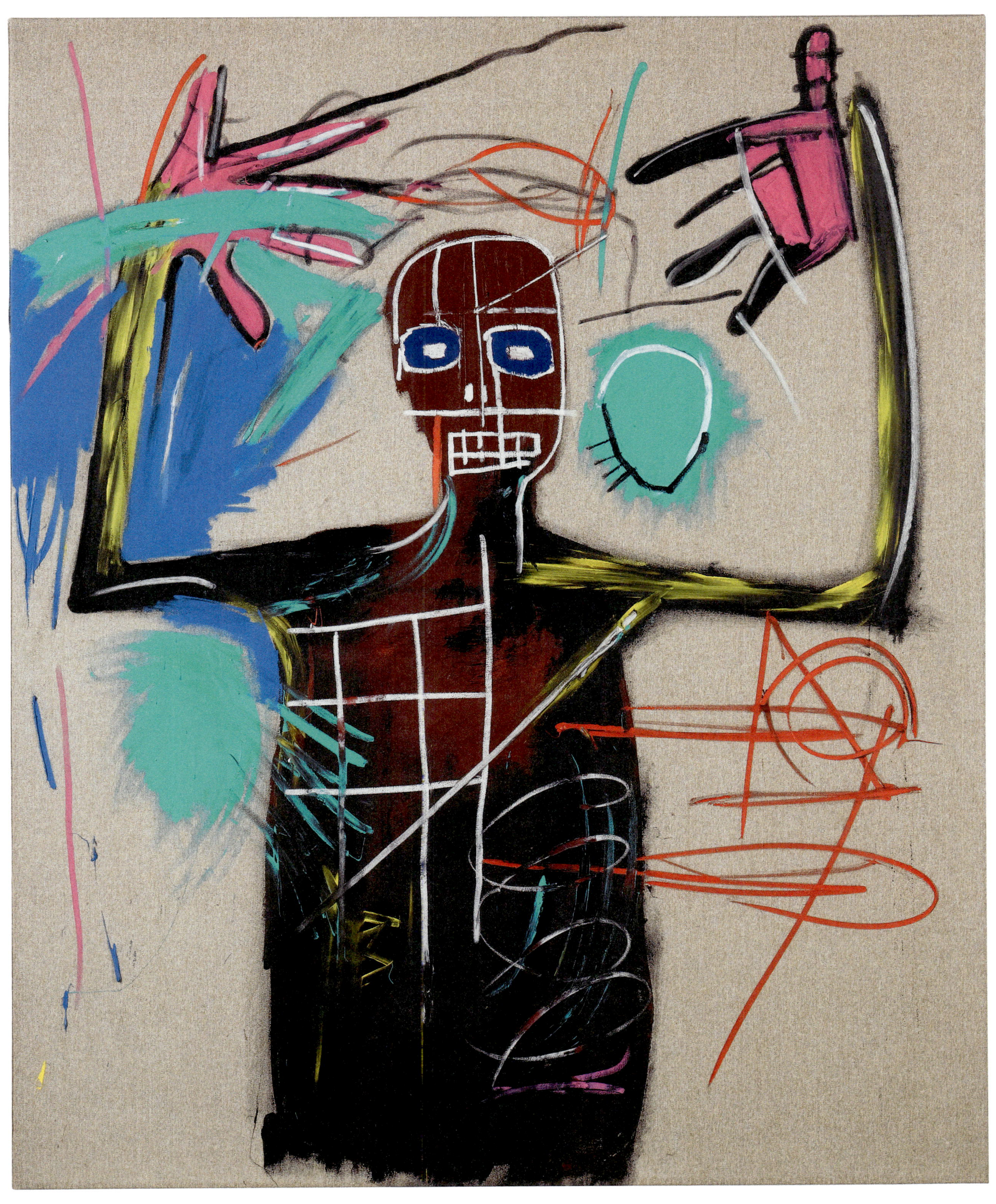

Punch Bag, 1983, 187 × 157 cm

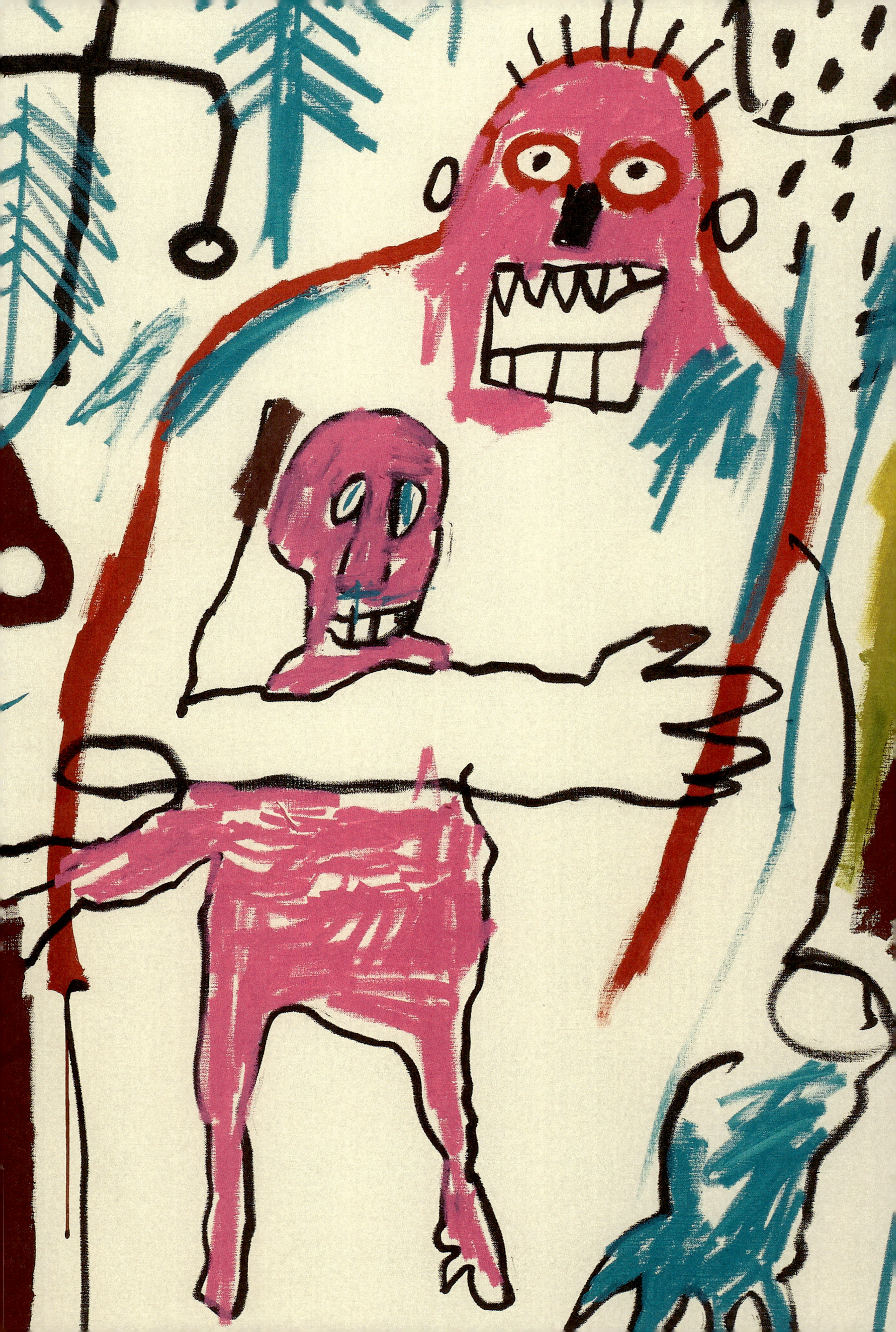

Foreword
Bruno Bischofberger

When curator and writer Dieter Buchhart called me this summer and told me that he had been invited by Iwan Wirth to help organize an exhibition about Jean-Michel Basquiat's time in Switzerland and the Engadin, and that he realized such a show would be unthinkable without my involvement, I initially was somewhat taken aback. After all, I've been contemplating just such a project for a very long time—yet I've never attempted it. Now, however, I am thrilled that Hauser & Wirth and Dieter have devoted themselves to the subject. To my delight, the exhibition is being held at the very same place in St. Moritz where, many years ago, I was the first to run a gallery.

The conversations I've been having with Dieter and others while searching my archives for photographs and looking through Jean-Michel's works (some of which I hadn't encountered for a long time)—caused many memories to come flooding back to me.

In May 1982, I became Jean-Michel's exclusive worldwide dealer, until his death in 1988. His frequent visits to us in Switzerland proved formative—not only for Jean-Michel, but also for me, my wife Yoyo, and our four children, Lea, Nina, Cora, and Magnus. I showed him everything that was important to me, and with his insatiable curiosity, he absorbed everything that was new to him. He was especially interested in art and my different collections. In addition to visual art, these consisted of photography; design, especially twentieth century; folk art, from both an artistic and an ethnographic point of view, made in Switzerland, Austria, Germany, and the other Alpine countries; and prehistoric stone objects from all over the world. Jean-Michel also showed a strong interest in Swiss history, cultural traditions, all kinds of music, or food and wine—and it didn't take long before he knew a great deal about all of it.

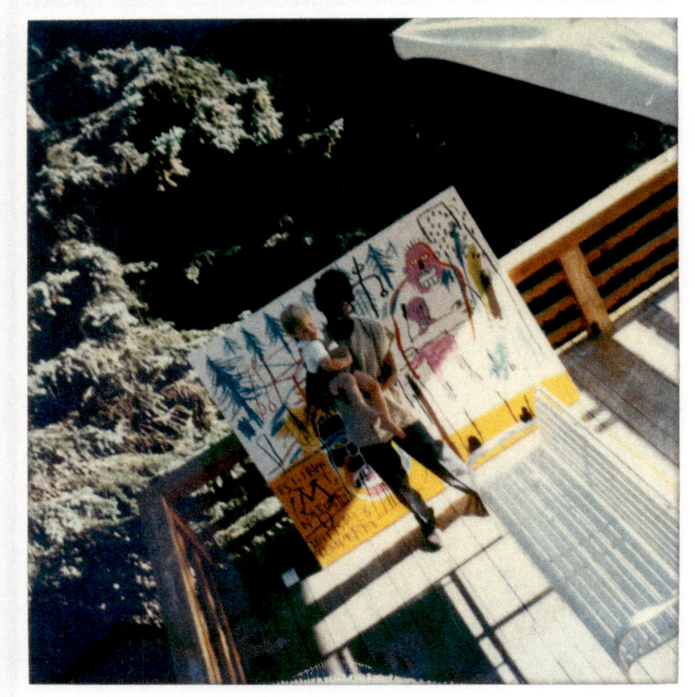

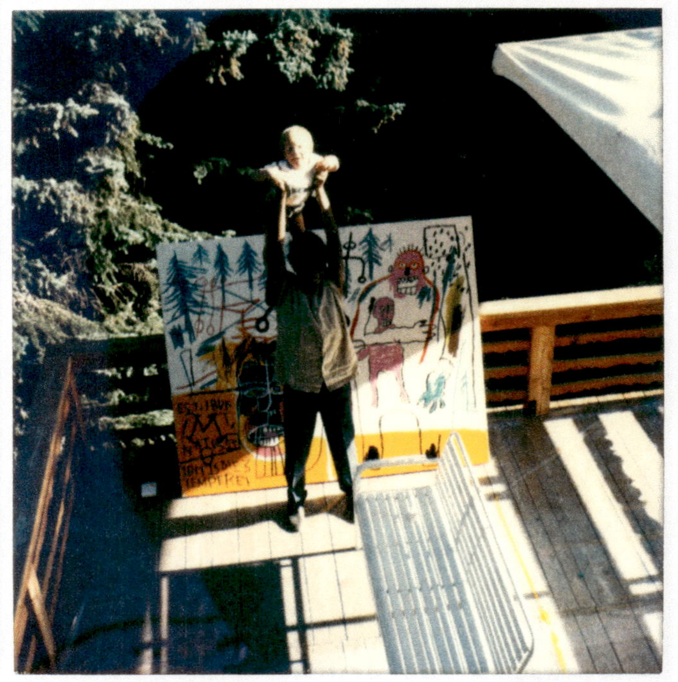

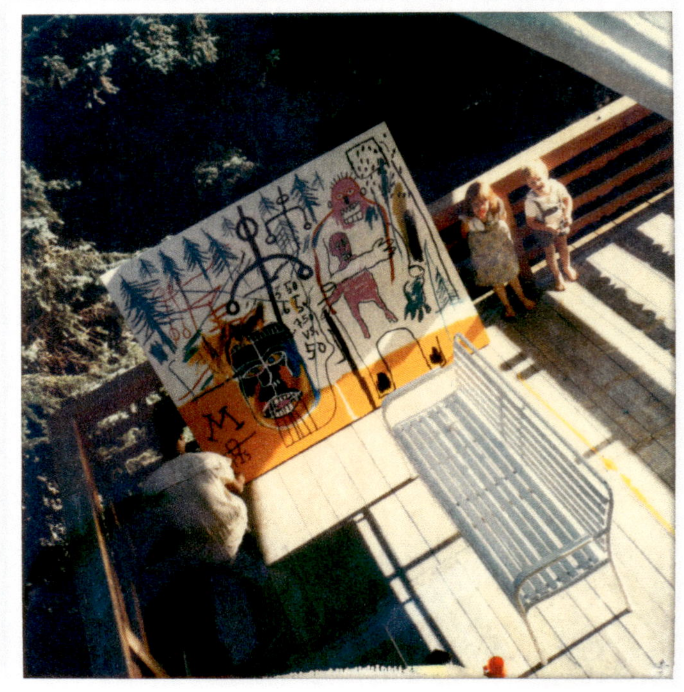

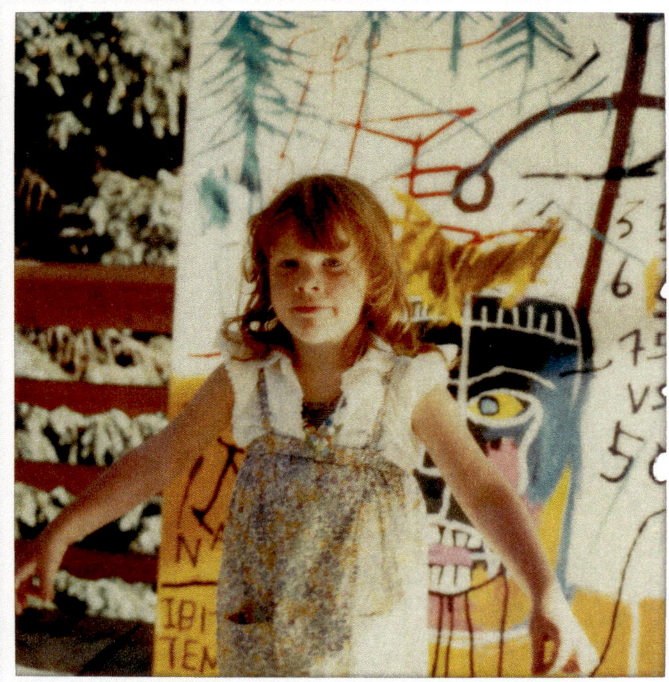

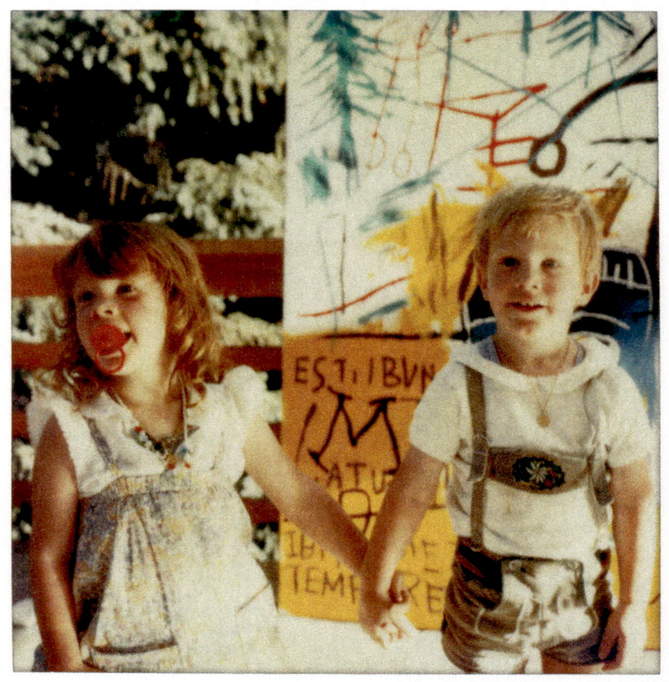

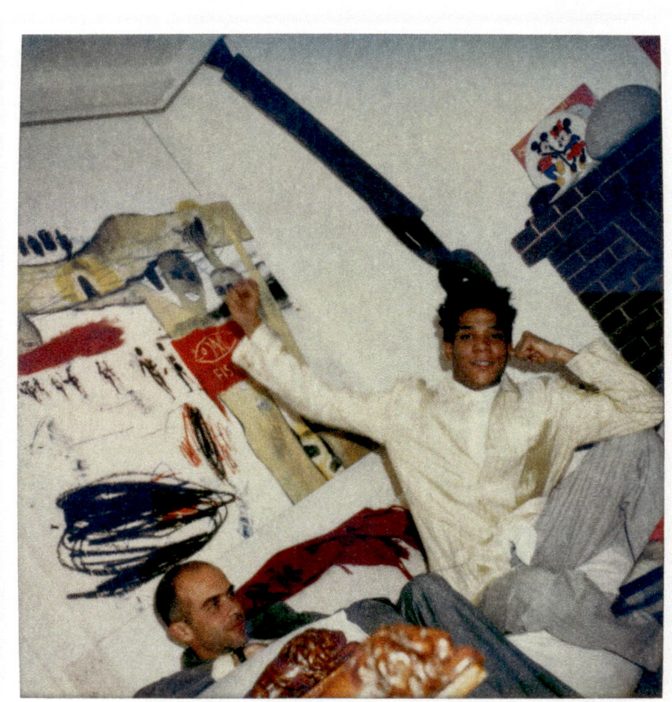

Opposite page:
Jean-Michel Basquiat and Magnus Bischofberger (top); Jean-Michel Basquiat and Cora and Magnus Bischofberger (bottom) in front of Basquiat's recently completed *Swiss Son* on the terrace of Chesa Lodisa, Bischofberger's house in St. Moritz, 1983

Above:
Cora Bischofberger (left); Cora and Magnus Bischofberger (right) in front of Basquiat's recently completed *Swiss Son* on the terrace of Chesa Lodisa, St. Moritz, 1983

Right:
Francesco Clemente and Jean-Michel Basquiat at Chesa Lodisa, St. Moritz, winter 1984–85

I learned a lot from him, too. On my first visit to his combination studio-apartment in New York, I asked him which artists had impressed and perhaps influenced him the most. The first thing he said was: "Works by very young children." I, too, admired and collected my own children's first creations. Of course, many had done so before me, especially artists. At the end of Picasso's life, for instance, the artist explained that he'd always tried to paint like little children, but never really succeeded.

Basquiat's visits to Switzerland, his trips to my home canton of Appenzell, and, above all, his longer stays with us at our holiday home, Chesa Lodisa, in St. Moritz, offered us more peace and time than was available during my visits to New York. Perhaps he appreciated that quality time together most of all—but of course the Engadin's extra-ordinary mountains and sheer beauty impacted him as well.

Jean-Michel's aura was radiant, and every-where he appeared, the Swiss were curious and interested in him. He, in turn, was always interested in them and our ancient Swiss traditions. In his work, Jean-Michel was ahead of his time; despite his young age, he was very radical and self-confi-dent. He was exceptionally intelligent, anticipated a great many developments, and influenced not only his contemporaries but artists throughout the following decades, up until the present day and no doubt beyond. Jean-Michel was a great artist, a fascinating interlocutor, and a wonderful friend to me, my wife, and my whole family. Hardly a day goes by when I don't think about him and still miss him.

I am very pleased to see some of the works that Jean-Michel created at our homes in the Engadin and in Switzerland appear together in this exhi-bition, as this is just as much a part of my own history. Many thanks to Hauser & Wirth for taking up this idea, and to Dieter Buchhart and Anna Karina Hofbauer for expertly shepherding this special exhibition.

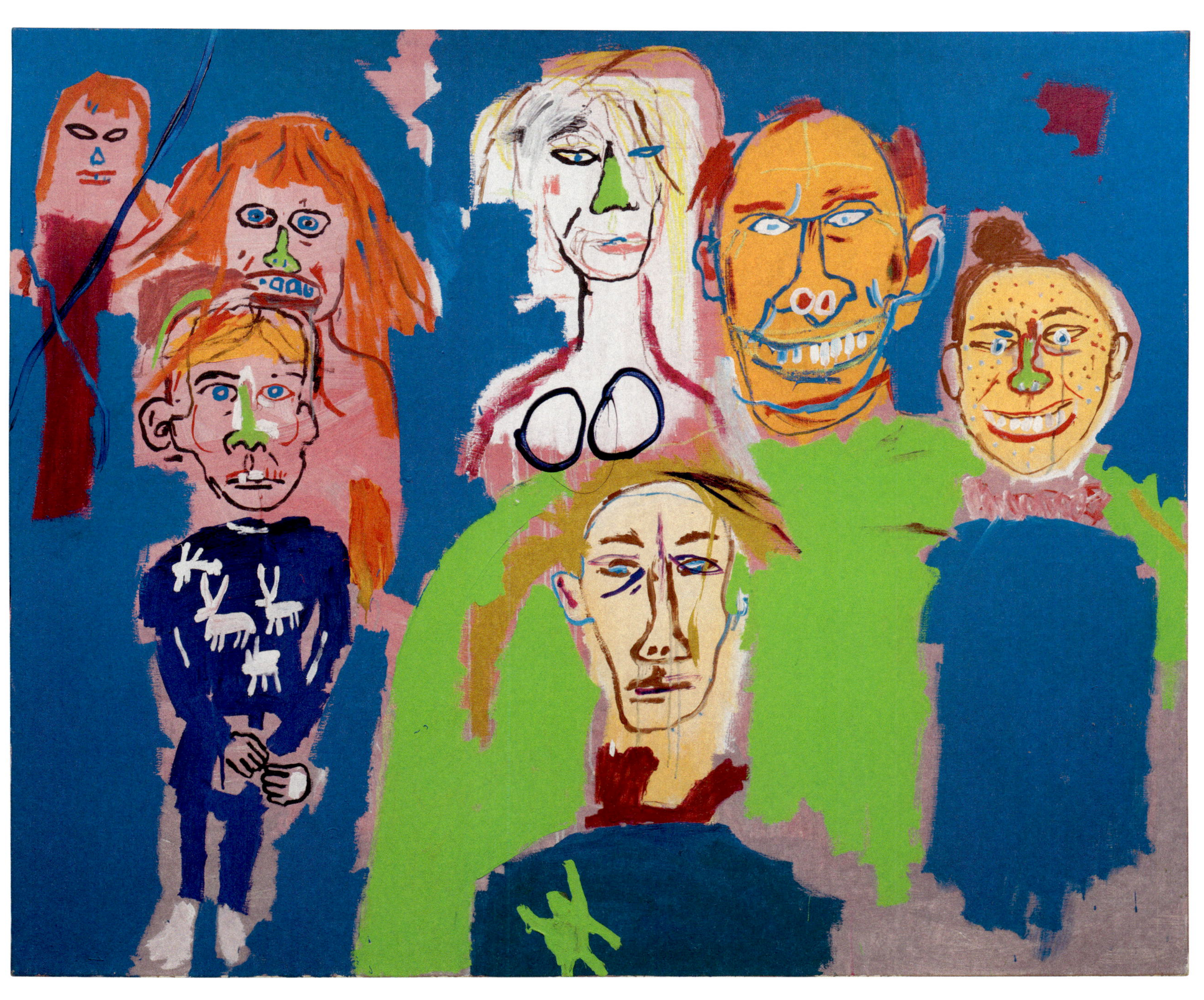

The Bischofbergers, 1984, 162 × 202 cm

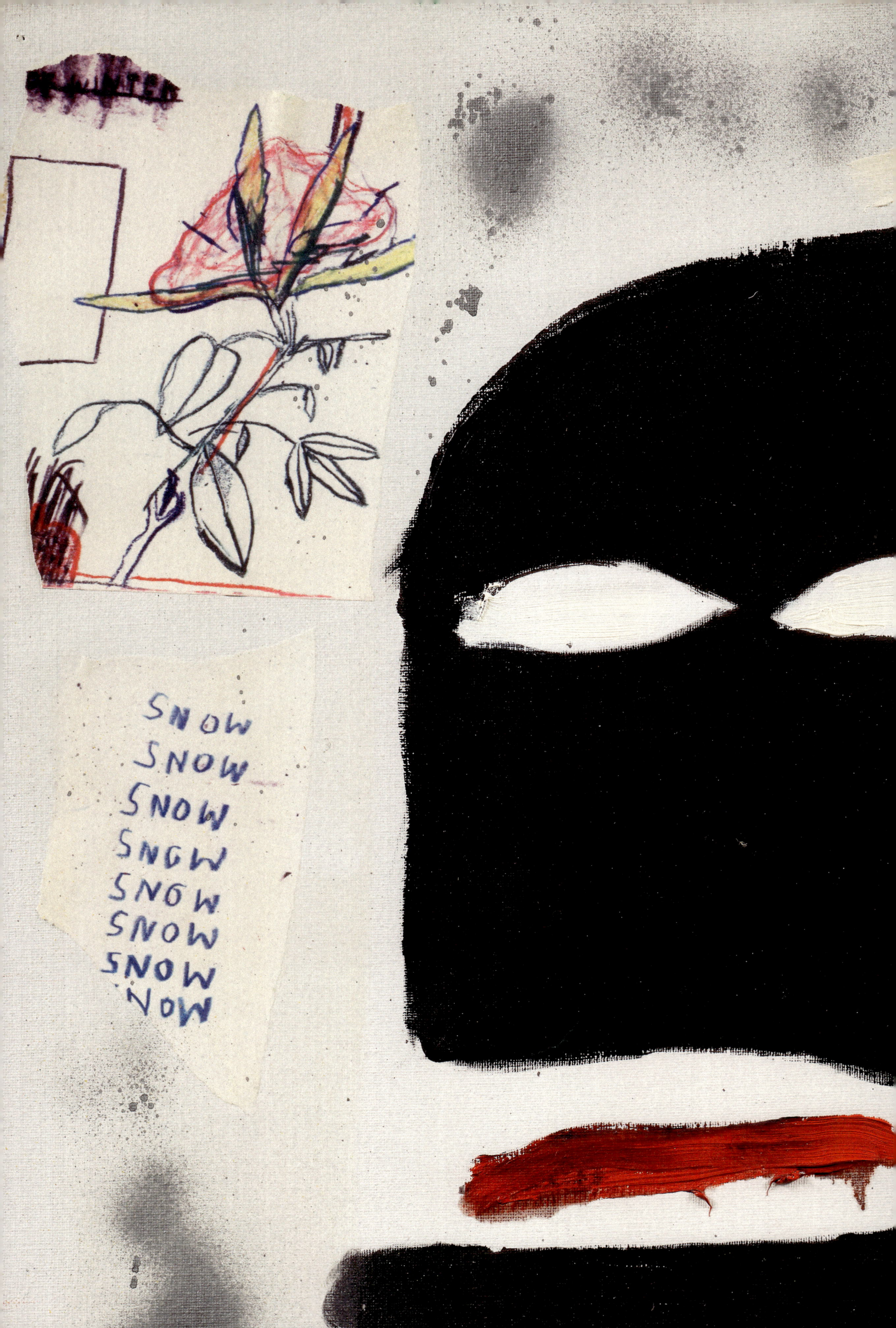
WINTER
SNOW
SNOW
SNOW
SNOW
SNOW
SNOW
SNOW
NOW

Basquiat in the Engadin
Dieter Buchhart

Mankind will learn, he suggested. They learn a little more slowly than He had assumed. "That's because the most competent among them will always try to change that small part of the world which they know. One of these days they'll discover the world instead of improving it, and not forget what they already discovered."[1]
—Sten Nadolny, *The Discovery of Slowness*

"I think the mystery of this mountain landscape is its light, its sun, and then, when it becomes more familiar, the infinite abundance of delightful details and the picturesque charm of a summer life," Swiss author Jakob Christoph Heer enthused in 1898 in his travel guide *Streifzüge im Engadin*, or *Exploring the Engadin*.[2] Almost one hundred years later, the famous New York artist Jean-Michel Basquiat was also unable to extricate himself from the "revelation of beauty" that makes it possible to forget the "enigma of existence," as Swiss poet Conrad Ferdinand Meyer put it in 1866.[3] Basquiat was enamored with the mountains, the ibexes, the ski lifts, the bratwurst, and the hospitality of the Bischofberger family. As Basquiat's gallerist Bruno Bischofberger later recalled, after they decided he would become Basquiat's art dealer, the artist would visit Bischofberger "in Switzerland often, which he especially liked. Around half a dozen times in Zurich and seven times in St. Moritz, four of those times in the summer."[4]

In his research, art critic Michel Nuridsany found that Basquiat traveled a total of fifteen times to Switzerland—to Zurich, Basel, and St. Moritz. In Zurich, he worked on paintings and drawings at the Bischofbergers' home, located in the village of Küsnacht, as well as in the storeroom of Bischofberger's gallery, in central Zurich. In St. Moritz, he worked at the Bischofbergers' holiday home, integrating motifs like ski lifts, pine trees, mountains, and bratwursts into his visual language.[5] In the works Basquiat created in the Engadin—

a region of Switzerland famous for its breathtaking Alpine panoramas and many preserved local traditions—the influence of the cultural and natural landscape is clearly legible.

With his symbolically laden, furiously executed, and highly complex works, Basquiat took New York's art world by storm in the 1980s. In 1982, he became one of the youngest artists ever to participate in the influential international exhibition Documenta, and he quickly became recognized as a key influence on and decisive innovator of the art of the 1980s. His influence continued to reverberate across the art of subsequent decades, and still does today. In less than a decade, he created around one thousand paintings, including more than 160 joint works with Andy Warhol,[6] and over two thousand drawings—a comprehensive oeuvre brimming with intensity and originality. In the process, the highly political artist, with his "inimitable stroke,"[7] used collage and assemblage to link figuration, language, and painting in an inimitable manner. Drawing was always the foundation of Basquiat's artistic practice,[8] though letters, words, lists, and phrases are often an integral part of his art. As gallerist and art critic Klaus Kertess fittingly notes: "In the beginning of his creation, there was the word. He loved words for their sense, for their sound, and for their look; he gave eyes, ears, mouth—and soul—to words."[9]

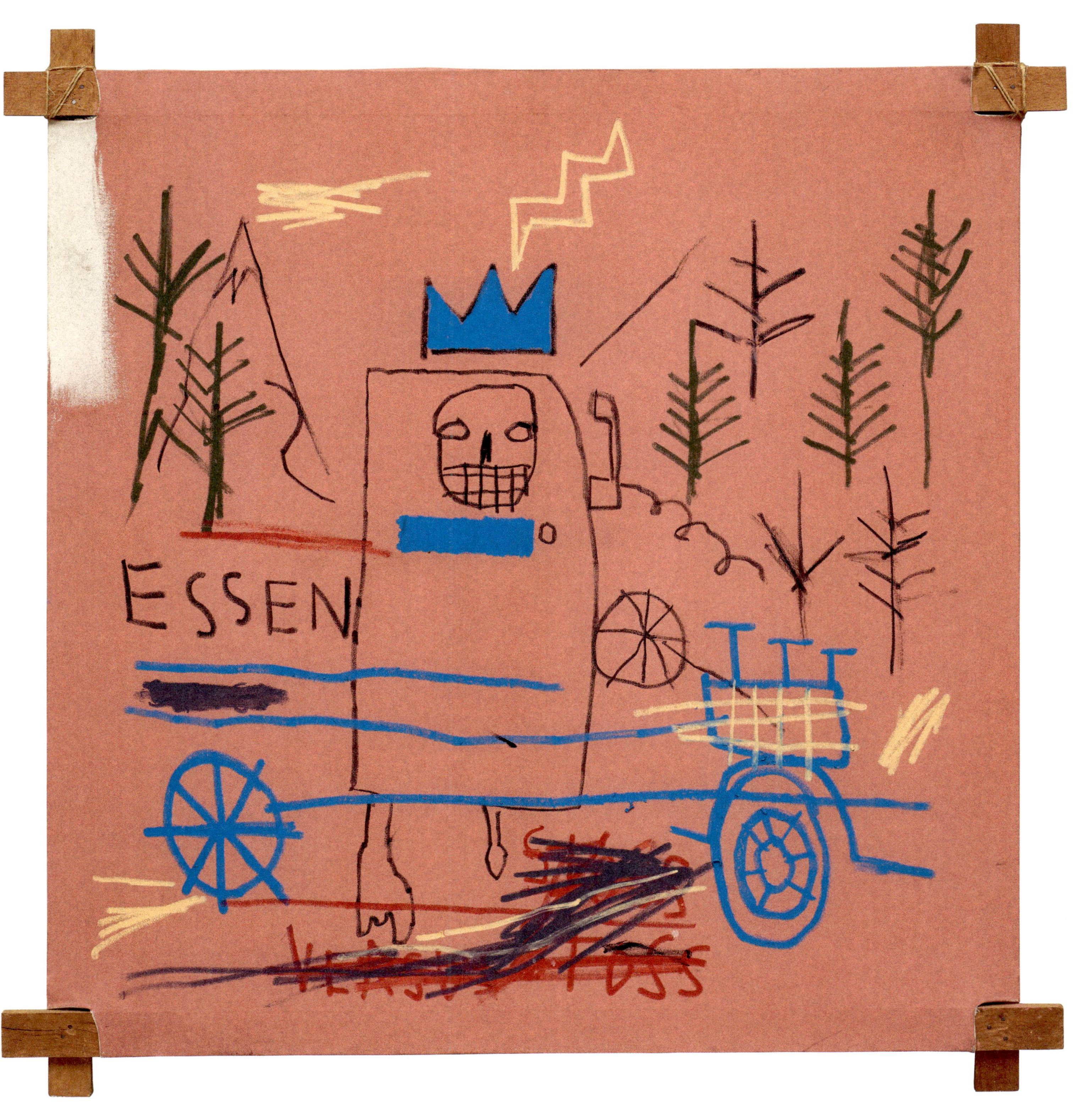

Bruno in Appenzell, 1982, 140 × 140 cm

1982

Certain factors clearly shaped Basquiat: the variety and intensity of the New York art world and its museums, the everyday racism he was confronted with, his urban environment, and the African diaspora. However, the influences of both the Engadin's unique landscape and the Bischofberger family also came to be reflected in various series of works. What emerges is a contrast between the pulsating life, nightclubs, street noise, and breakneck speed of the metropolis of New York and the artist's "discovery of slowness"[10] in the unique, awe-inspiring landscape of the Engadin, where "the colorful consequence of extremely significant geographical developments over a vast period of time resulted in the formation of the most unique mountainous region in the world."[11]

These influences are unmistakable already in *The Dutch Settlers* (1982; pp. 20–21). This monumental major work, consisting of nine canvases, combines a wide range of cutting-edge elements. Here Basquiat creates one of his significant *Wissensräume* (spaces of knowledge), reflecting the field of tension of concrete poetry, the "cut-up" technique of Beat writer William S. Burroughs, and the *Sprechgesang* (speak-singing) of hip-hop. Basquiat distilled not only language but his entire surroundings and humankind's collective memory and knowledge: "He picks up books, cereal boxes, the newspaper or whatever is around. He finds a word or phrase and paints it on his board or canvas."[12] The combination of pentimento, acrylic paint, and oil stick in *The Dutch Settlers* results in a form of painted hip-hop. It shows how Basquiat's knowledge-based artistic strategies raised the same sort of questions that would come to shape the contextual art of the 1990s and the present, rather than exploring the formal and stylistic issues related to the Neo-expressionism of the 1980s. The artist creates a space of knowledge with an internal logic that can unlock new spaces of thought for the viewer. Creating such "montages" of canvases opened up yet another innovative avenue, allowing Basquiat to assemble various visual fields by combining and recombining the paintings—literally, by sampling them. For example, for *Flesh and Spirit* (1982–83), he combined up to twelve panels while granting each one its own autonomy. He thus created "eye rap,"[13] assembling various words, signs, pictograms, and visual elements with and against one another.

The various elements of *The Dutch Settlers* also denote manifold political and social issues. With the word "TOBACCO" in all caps, Basquiat refers to slavery and exploitation in the production of raw materials, in the cultivation and harvesting of this valuable crop, while marking the stylized Black individual depicted below with an arrow and the word "NUBIA"—again written in all caps and crossed out—a reference to the Nubia region, which straddles the Nile and is considered the birthplace of African civilization.[14] With a crown and copyright emblem, Basquiat emphasizes the anonymized individual as a stylized hero of his works. The word "SAMSON" on the next panel, again written in all caps, and then repeated and crossed out, refers to the biblical figure identified with the enslaved, whose hair—the source of his strength—was cut off.[15] Here, the artist takes a stand against complacency through these words, deletions, signs, symbols, and figures. "Wielding his brush as a weapon,"[16] Basquiat fought against exploitation, consumer society, oppression, racism, and police violence. He likewise uses words, like his brushstrokes, as a weapon. "That's all words, they're all I have"[17]—playwright and novelist Samuel Beckett's words seem to echo in Basquiat's radical artistic legacy.

We most clearly see Basquiat's reference to the Engadin and its "revelation of beauty" in the two pine trees on the second and third panels from the left, the latter of which also includes an ibex, an animal native to the Engadin that is also found in the coat of arms of the canton Grisons as well as on two carved sixteenth-century chests kept in the Bischofbergers' home in St. Moritz. A mountain road appears in the fifth panel, united through the artist's "eye rap" with both anatomical representations and geographical maps, ending on the last panel with a notary seal, which seems to certify the legitimacy of his space of knowledge. Finally, the figure in the first panel may be a portrait of Bischofberger, his gallerist and host, which a comparison to *Swiss Son* (1983; p. 22) seems to confirm.

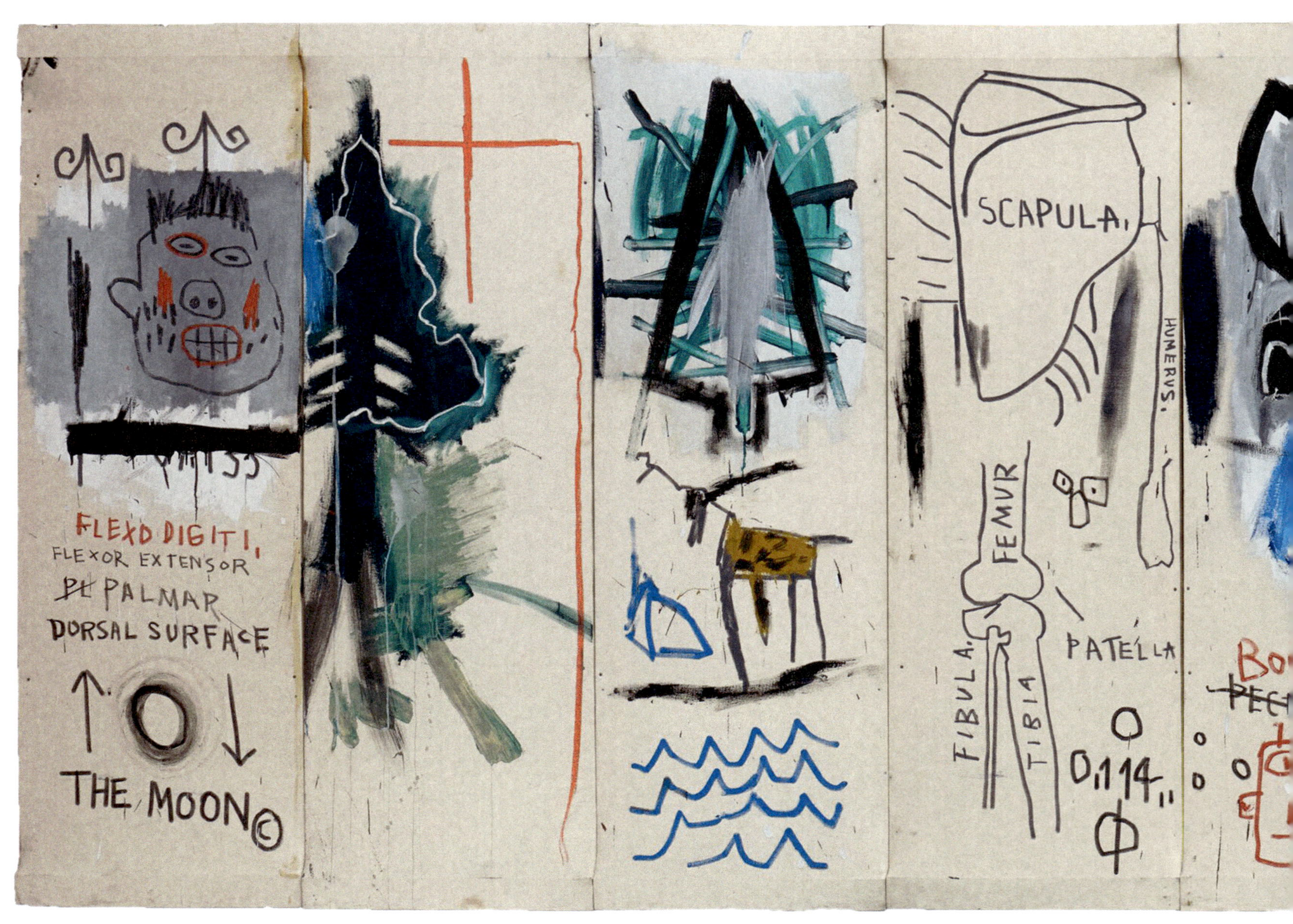

The Dutch Settlers, 1982, 183 × 549 cm

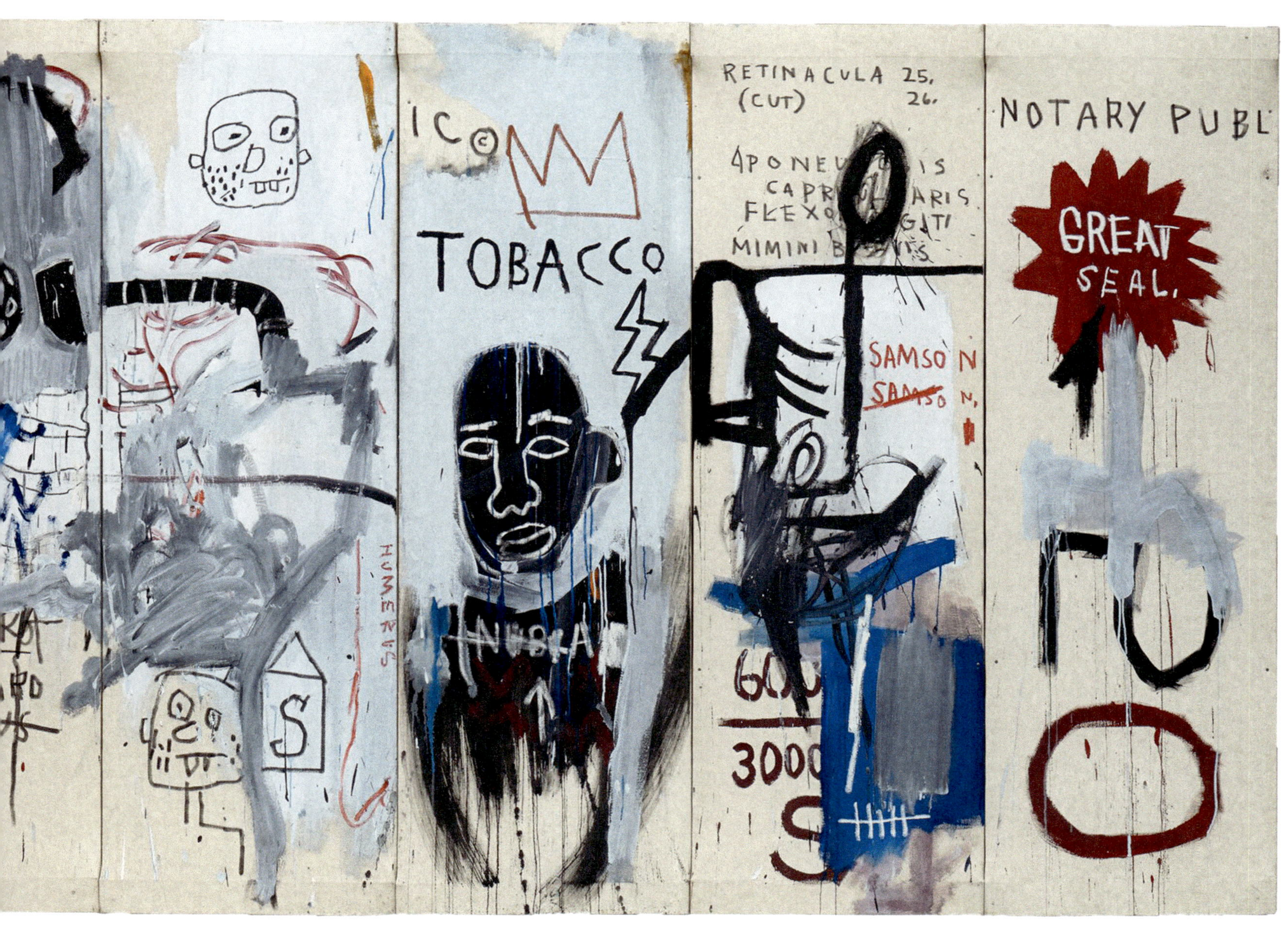

IC ©
TOBACCO
HOMERUS
S
RETINACULA 25,
(CUT) 26.
APONEU IS
CAPR ARIS
FLEXO G T
MIMINI B
SAMSO N
SAM SO N,
600
3000
S
NOTARY PUBL
GREAT
SEAL.

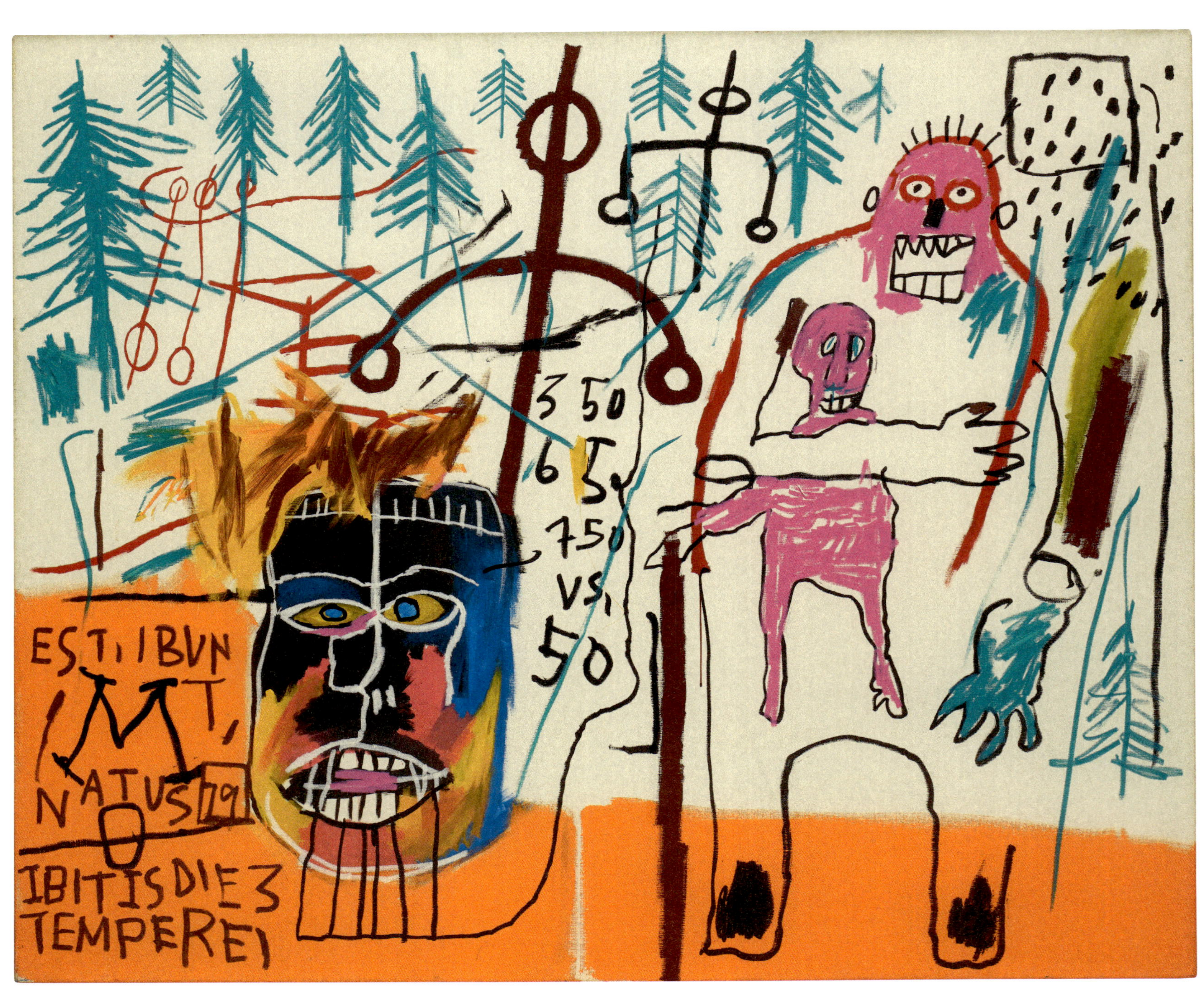

Swiss Son, 1983, 160 × 200 cm

Basquiat's first encounter with Bischofberger took place in late 1981, when the art dealer was visiting Annina Nosei Gallery in New York. He had already seen Basquiat's works at the *New York/New Wave* exhibition, at P.S.1 in Long Island City, after the show's curator, Diego Cortez, had mentioned the artist's work to him. Bischofberger recounts the meeting:

> So I went to the basement with [Nosei], and there was this person in the corner. I realized it was Basquiat painting something, but she went out with me again afterward, and he didn't come over to say hello. I didn't go there either to say hello because I just wanted to be discreet. I didn't ask her, "Could you please introduce me?" We just went off again. Basquiat later on told me, "Oh, I realized immediately who you were, but I was angry at you because I heard you compared my work with Twombly and Dubuffet, which is really not true." … I didn't mean it to be disrespectful, or that he's a rip-off of those. I just saw something in the same spirit. So that's where I first saw him. That was probably in November or December of 1981.[18]

From there, things progressed quickly:

> In May 1982, a few months later, when I heard that Basquiat had left Annina Nosei Gallery because of certain disagreements, I visited him at his first studio on Crosby Street, where he had just moved in. We agreed that I would hold a show of his work in Zurich in the early fall and that effective immediately I would be his art dealer.[19]

In September 1982, Basquiat, together with his assistant Stephen Torton, made his first trip to Zurich, a weeklong sojourn to mark his first solo exhibition at Galerie Bruno Bischofberger. When, to the artist's disappointment, Bischofberger didn't host an opening reception, the gallerist made it up to Basquiat by taking the pair to his hometown of Appenzell, in the mountains.[20] "I remember driving along the road in the Mercedes and Bruno offered us a joint," recalls Torton.

He was just such a sophisticated guy, and he brought it out at the perfect moment. We smoked the pot as we were driving down a country road. They went to a local carnival, where a Felliniesque village scene took place. There was this bumper car thing set up on the mountain. So we got in and bought forty rides' worth of coins. And we were riding in the bumper cars and bashing into Bruno. And all of a sudden, it seemed like the whole village came out, and sort of ganged up on Jean-Michel.[21]

Basquiat's first contact with the overwhelming world of the mountains manifested itself briefly thereafter in the painting *Bruno in Appenzell* (1982; p. 17), which the artist dedicated to his Swiss gallerist and gave him as a present. In this work, Basquiat seeks to emphasize words precisely by deleting them: "I cross out words so you will see them more; the fact that they are obscured makes you want to read them."[22] For example, in *Bruno in Appenzell*, the words that were so vigorously crossed out virtually demand to be deciphered. Although difficult to decode, in the lower part of the painting, written in red, we can make out the words "STOSS VERSUS STOSS," once again in all caps. Here, Basquiat refers to the Stoss, a mountain pass in the canton Appenzell Ausserrhoden that connects Appenzellerland to the St. Gallen Rhine Valley. But it is, above all, a reference to the Battle of Stoss Pass in 1405, where the Appenzellers deftly defeated the Habsburgs, despite being massively outnumbered. This decisive battle, today still celebrated as a symbol of Appenzellers' freedom, piqued Basquiat's interest as a metaphor for victory against the oppressor.[23]

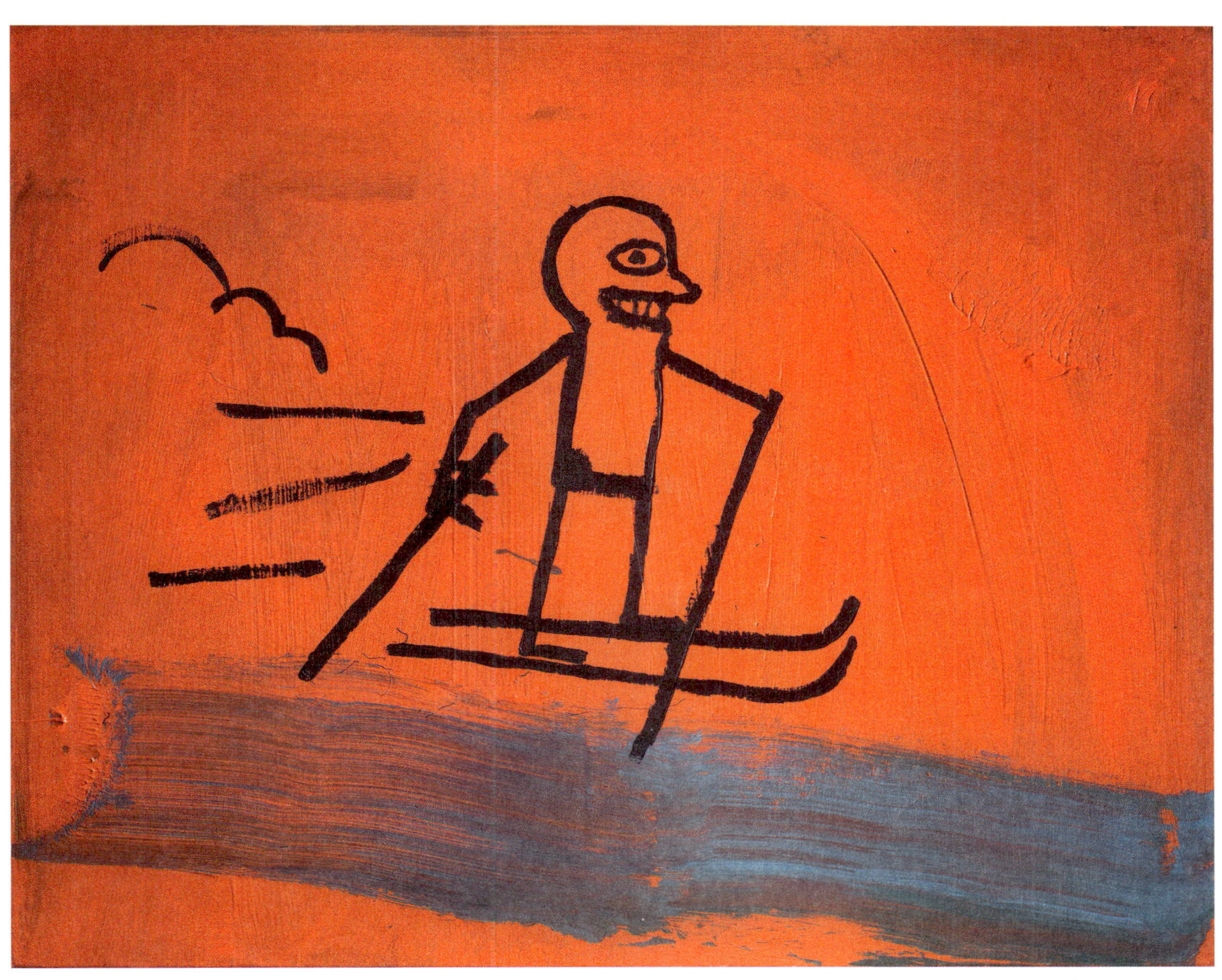

Skifahrer (Skier), 1983, 70 × 90 cm

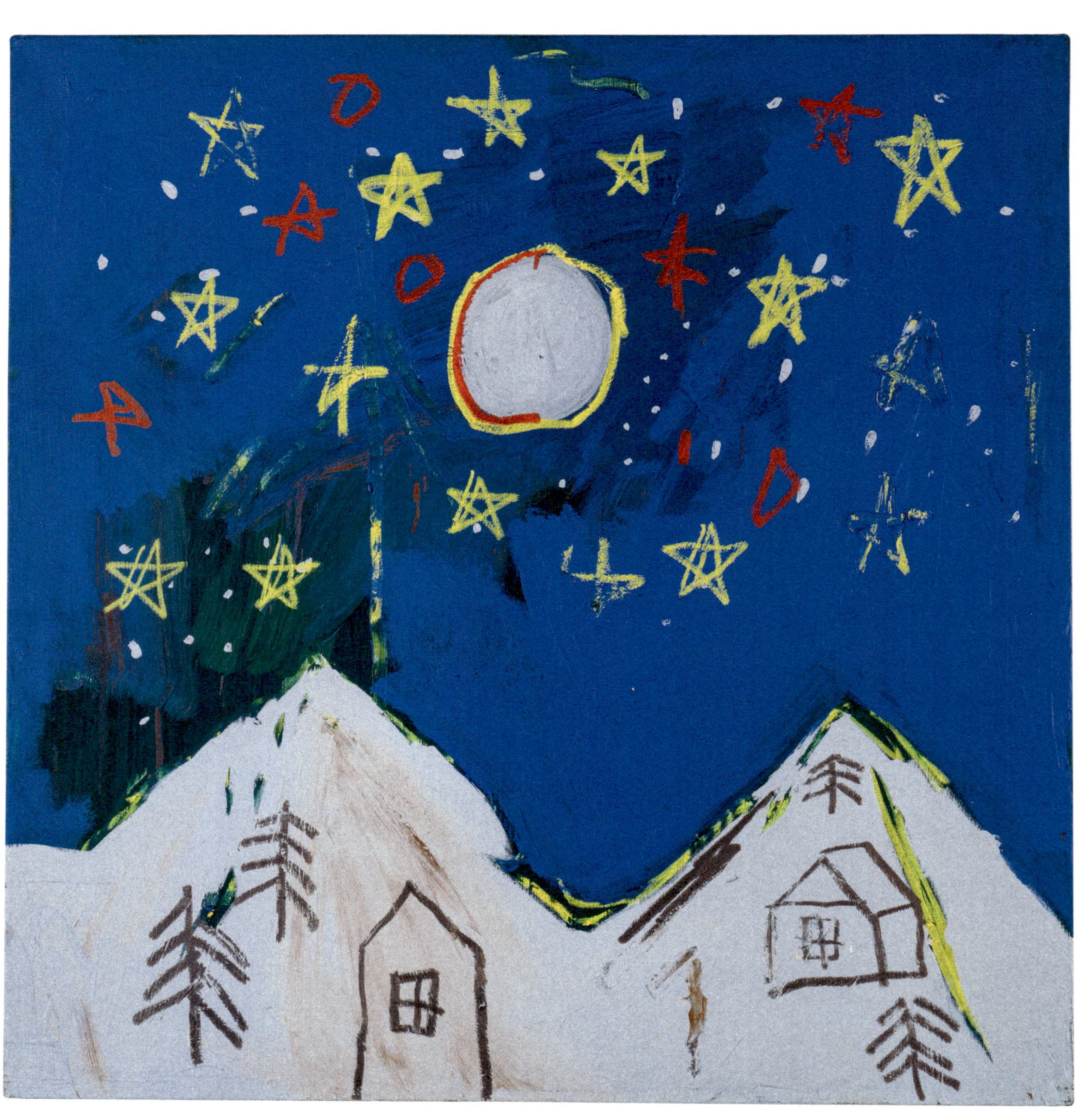

Nachtleben (Nightlife), 1983, 100 × 100 cm

1983

Basquiat took several trips to Switzerland, and to St. Moritz in particular, in 1983. Besides his solo show at Galerie Bruno Bischofberger in late September,[24] he also participated in group exhibitions at the legendary Galerie Beyeler in Basel—one of them, *Expressive Malerei nach Picasso* (Expressive Painting after Picasso)[25]—and at Kunstmuseum Luzern. Most of the works Basquiat created in the Engadin were probably made that same year.

Four groups can be discerned. First are the works that engage directly with the Engadin in a narrow sense, and which Basquiat intended to be hung, as if in a "hunting lodge," in the Bischofbergers' St. Moritz dining room.[26] This cycle includes *Skifahrer* (Skier; p. 25), *Nachtleben* (Nightlife; p. 26), *See* (Lake; p. 28), *Alpendorf* (Alpine Village; p. 29), and *Swiss House on Fire* (all 1983). The works share a simplified, cartoonish visual language on a largely monochromatic pictorial ground. For example, in *Alpendorf*, the Alpine village of the title is drawn on top of and scratched into partially wet green paint, while a reddish-brown colored bar just beneath the upper edge alludes to a horizon and sky. Similarly, in *Skifahrer*, Basquiat added the comic-like figure of a skier with just a few brushstrokes on a vermilion background. In *Swiss House on Fire*, we see the yellow outlines of the house, the fire, and the all-caps phrase "SWISS HOUSE ON FIRE ©," rendered in oil stick on a black ground.

The second group of works revolves around the subjects of the bull show and bratwurst—elements of Swiss culture that the artist encountered during an excursion with Bischofberger, as the gallerist reports:

> I once drove with the artist directly from the airport, where I had picked him up, to Neu St. Johann, where the Toggenburg Bull Show was taking place that day. In the Sidwald neighborhood, several bulls stood on a field to be evaluated and awarded prizes. Basquiat loved the atmosphere, the monumental bulls, the traditionally dressed, primeval, proud farmers. I sat with a few [of them] at the

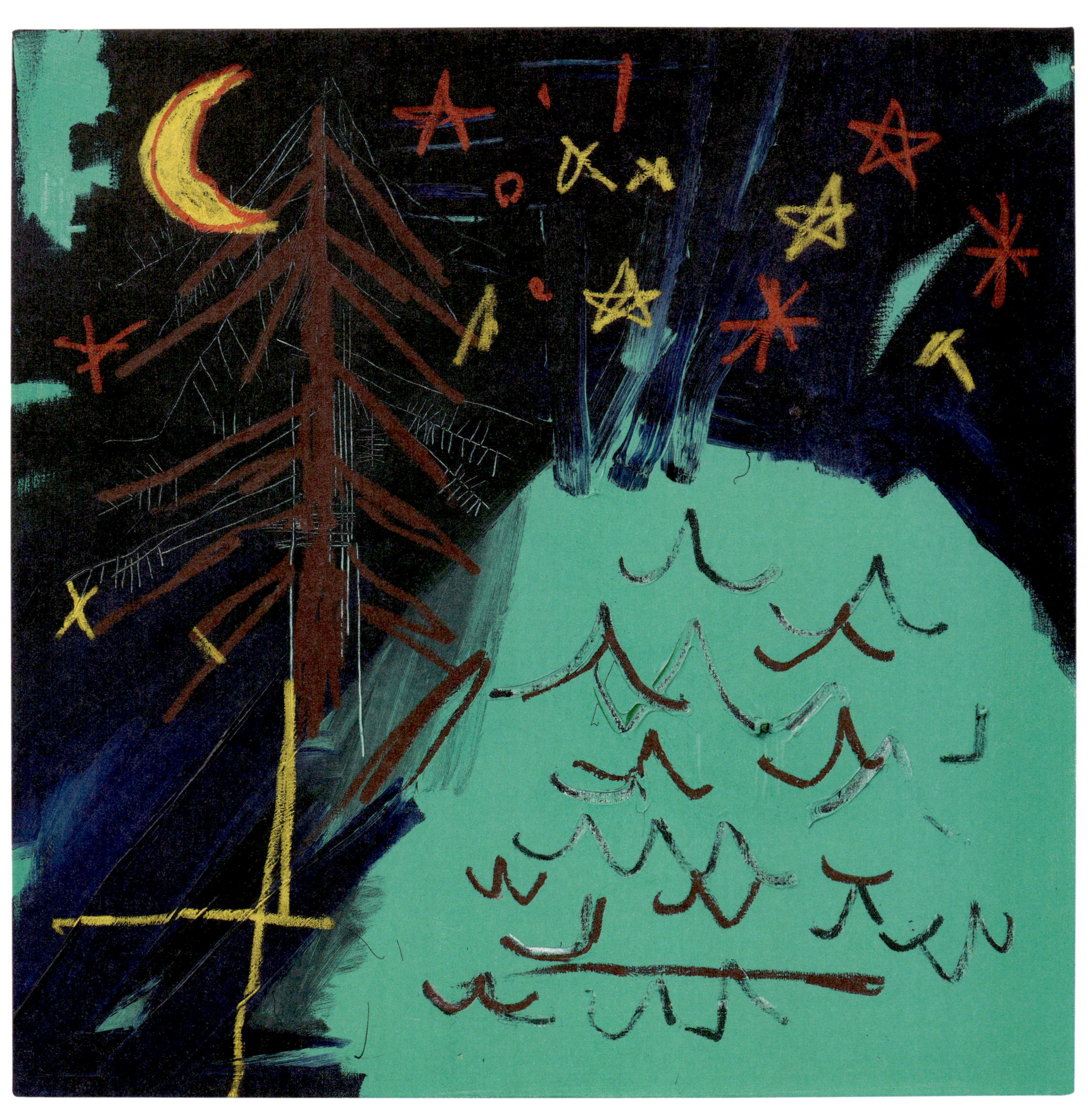

See (Lake), 1983, 101 × 101 cm

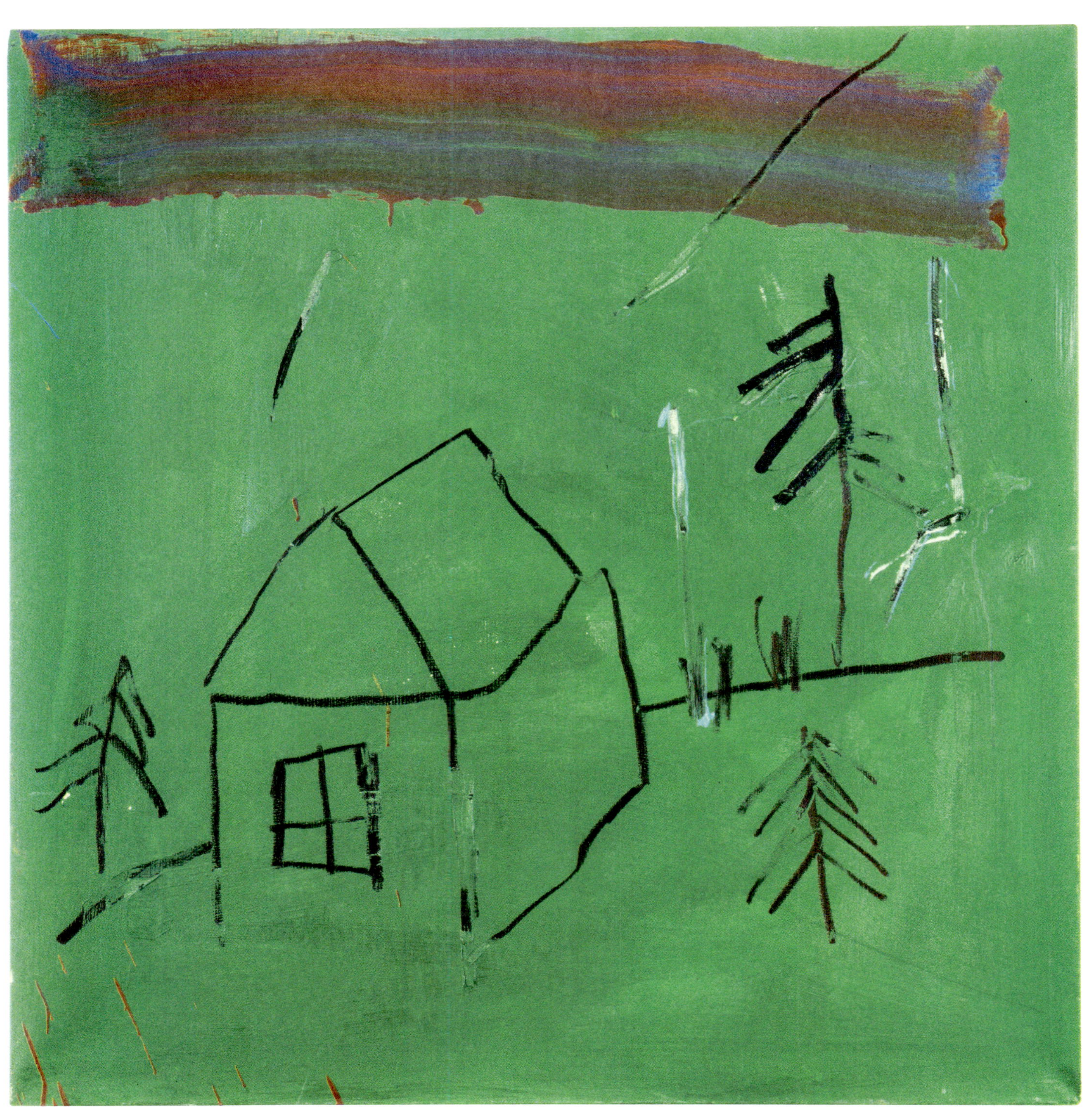

Alpendorf (Alpine Village), 1983, 102 × 102 cm

Gemsli pub and we started playing cards.
Basquiat was very tired. We were able
to get a room for him on the floor above and
he retreated there. But instead of sleeping,
he completed four fantastic color drawings
on the subject of the livestock show
[pp. 31–35]. He then returned to the smoky
pub and placed the large roll with the
drawings on the table, and it rolled open.
They showed bulls, bratwursts, and
many impressions of the event were inter-
woven, for example, the menu: "Schweins-
voressen, Kutteln, Bürli, etc."[27]

Alongside these elements from Switzerland, the
artist portrays several themes from American
film and culture. In so doing, Basquiat here combines
his "spaces of knowledge." Among the several
words that appear in all caps is the dominant word
"BRATWURST," which appears next to the logo
of the satire magazine *MAD* and a rendering of Alfred
E. Neuman, a recurring *MAD* character. The
canvases are also peppered with questions like
"WHICH MOVIE WITH LIZ TAYLOR?"; the notion
of the "ECLIPSE"; impressions of the bull show; the
sign of the local pub;[28] the nearly complete
"menu of the ox";[29] and words like "COWSHIT"
and "CHAINED NECK."
      The third grouping of Swiss works involves
depictions of the Bischofberger family. The two
portraits of Bischofberger's wife, Yoyo—both titled
Yoyo (Portrait of Christina Bischofberger) (1983;
pp. 38–39)—comparable with the hunting lodge
works, are stylized with pink oil stick on an iri-
descent background, with specks of red paint to
represent his subject's freckles. The even more
monumental canvas *Swiss Son* was created that
same year on the terrace of Chesa Lodisa,
Bischofberger's house in St. Moritz. In it, Bruno
looms like a behemoth, with a wide-open
mouth, while holding his son Magnus in his arms,
depicted against the wooded landscape of the
Engadin, including a ski lift.
      With *Punch Bag* (1983; p. 7), Basquiat created
a canvas markedly different from the other painted
works, and thus we can classify it in a fourth cate-
gory. It features an experimental application of

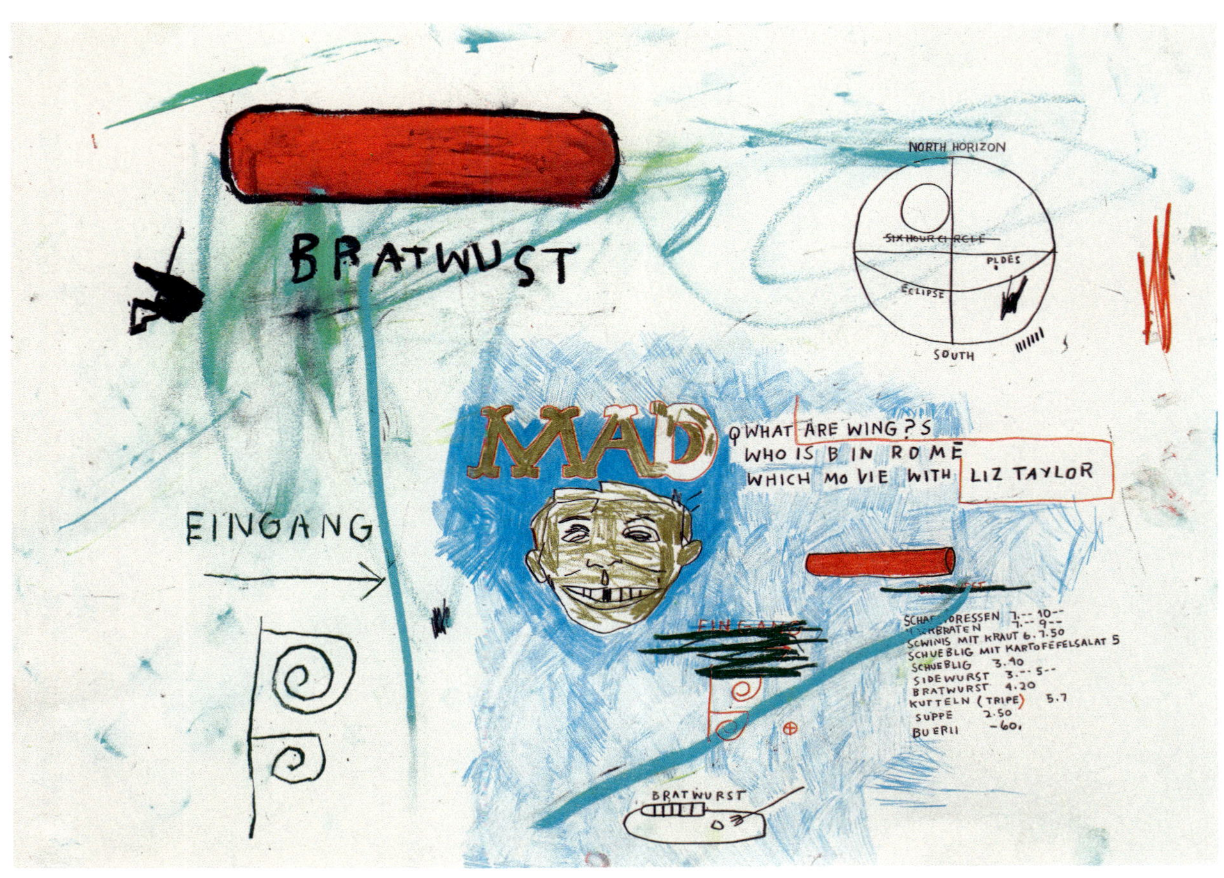

Bull Show One, 1983, 51 × 73 cm

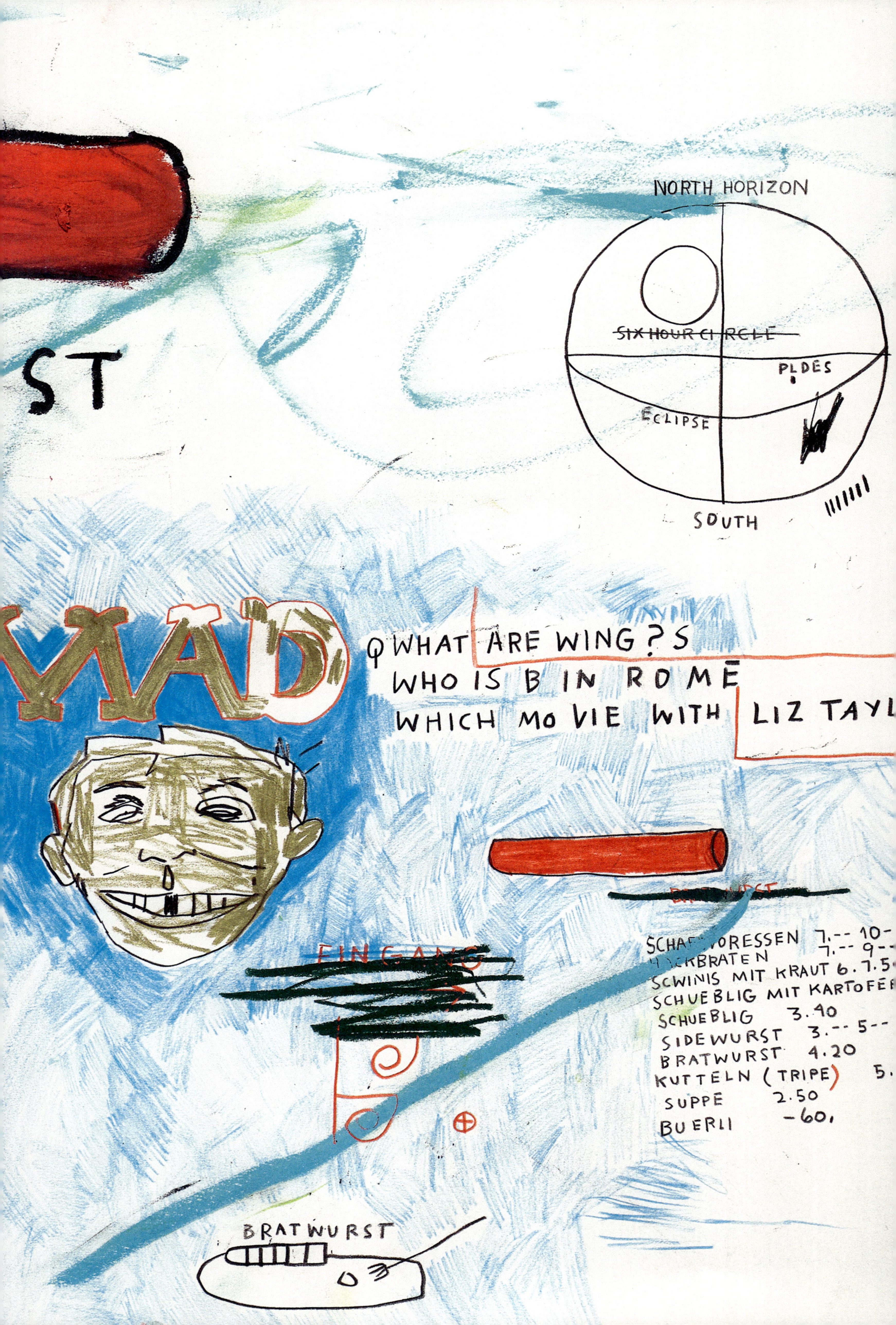

NORTH HORIZON
SIX HOUR CIRCLE
PLDES
ECLIPSE
SOUTH
ST
WAD
Q WHAT ARE WING? S
WHO IS B IN ROME
WHICH MO VIE WITH LIZ TAYL
EINGANG
SCHAFVORESSEN 7.-- 10-
HACKBRATEN 7.-- 9--
SCWINIS MIT KRAUT 6. 7.5
SCHUEBLIG MIT KARTOFE
SCHUEBLIG 3.40
SIDEWURST 3.-- 5--
BRATWURST 4.20
KUTTELN (TRIPE) 5.
SUPPE 2.50
BUERLI -60,
BRATWURST

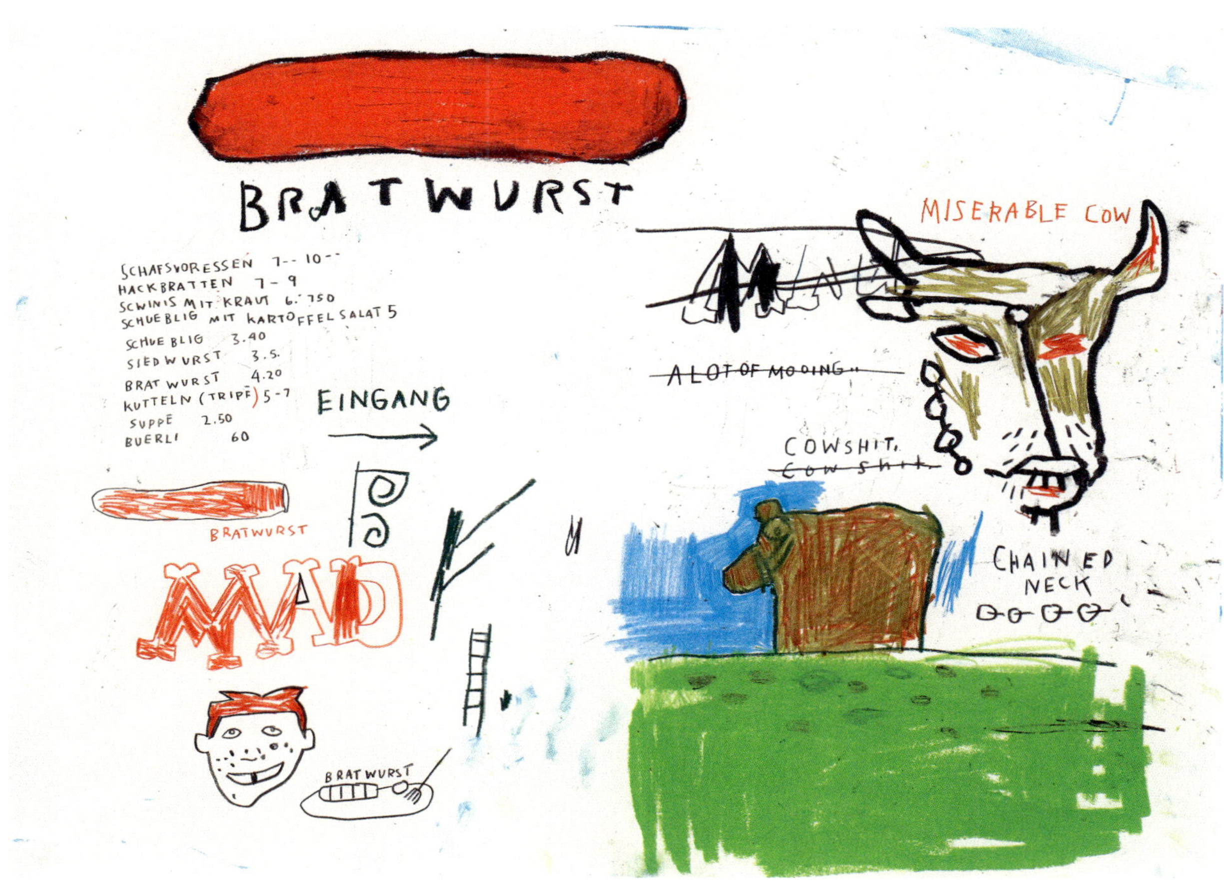

Bull Show Two, 1983, 51 × 73 cm

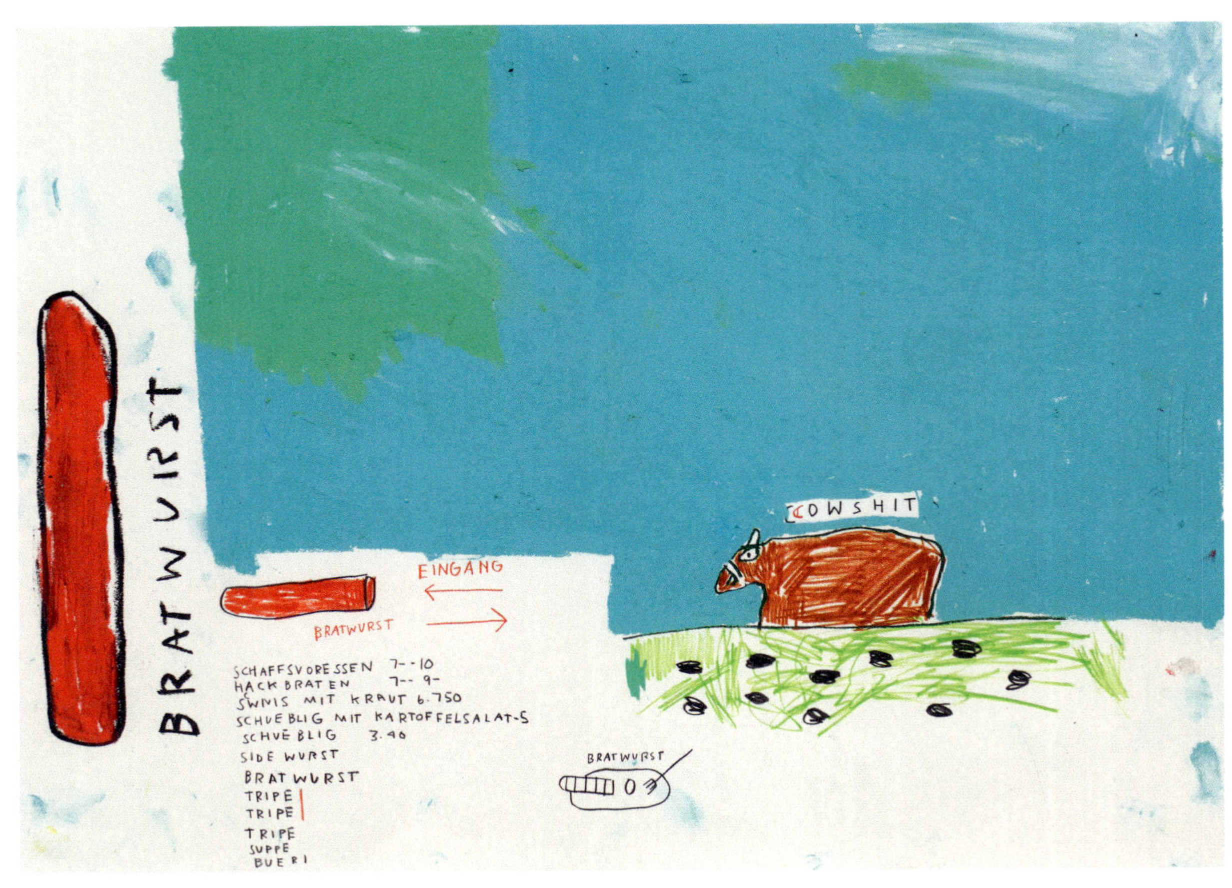

Bull Show Three, 1983, 51 × 73 cm

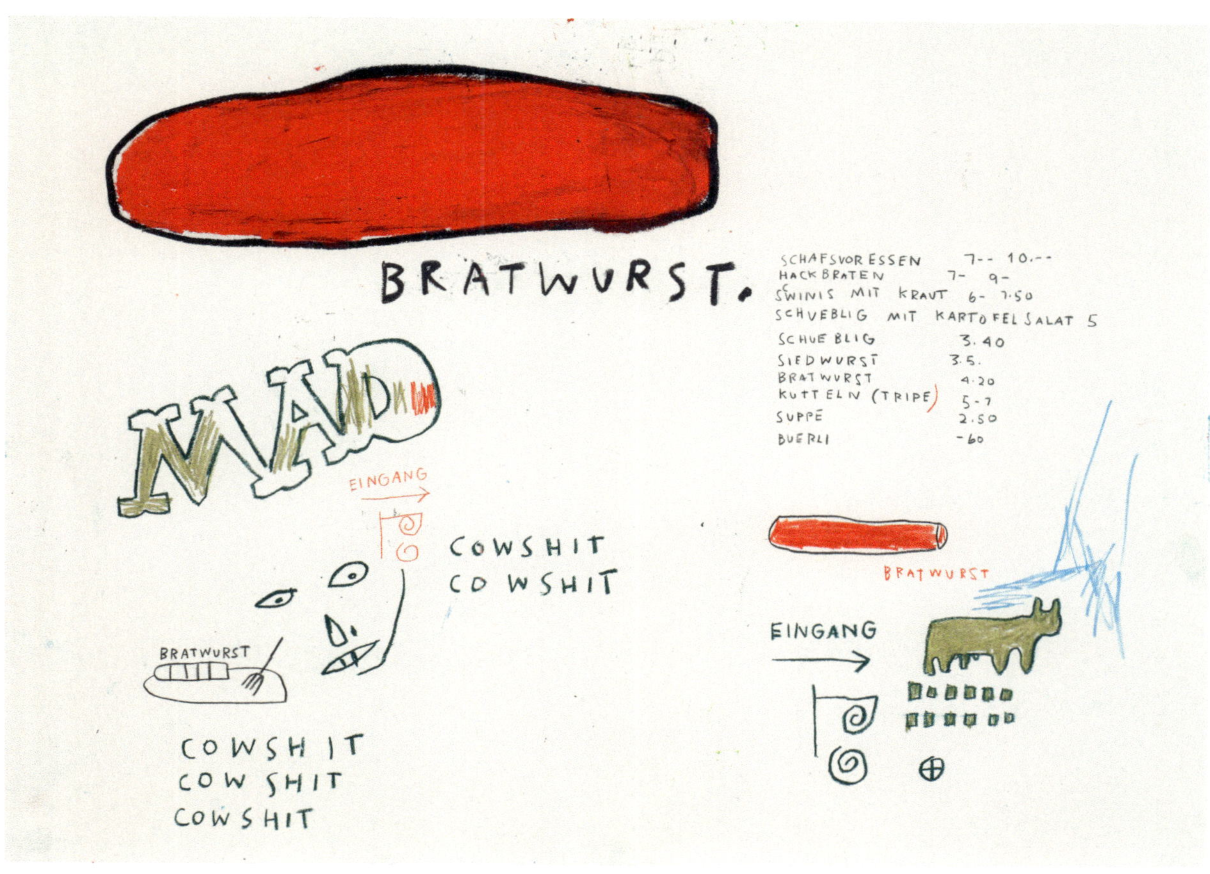

Bull Show Four, 1983, 51 × 73 cm

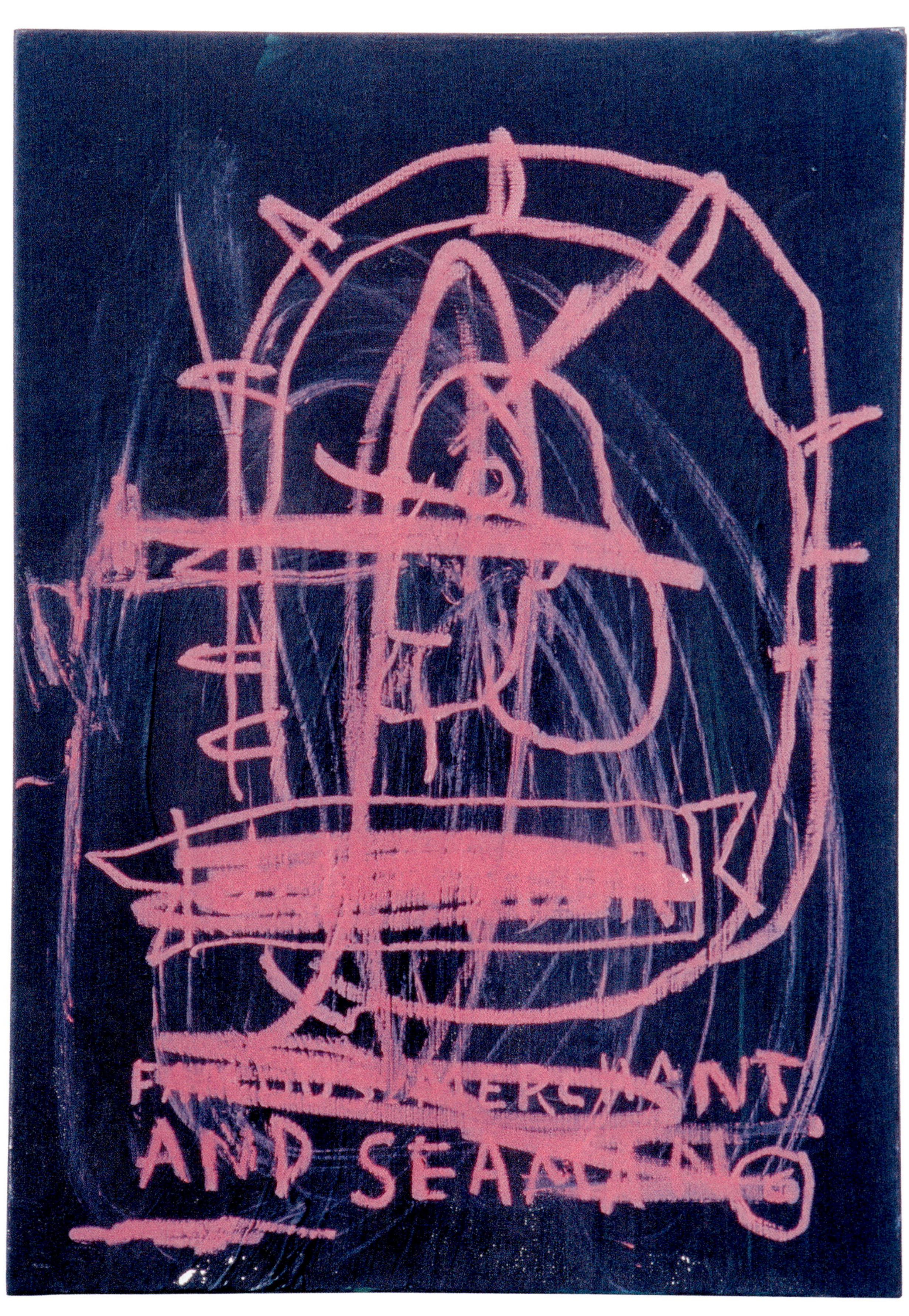

Famous Merchant and Seaman, 1983, 70 × 50 cm

acrylic paint with fingers and various broad brushes, as well as oil stick. The person of color depicted here—perhaps a self-portrait—has his hands up. The reflection of the self becomes a mirror of the everyday, oscillating between self-confidence, self-empowerment, and the racial discrimination Basquiat, as a Black man, was subject to and witnessed in his daily life.

That year, 1983, was also the year of Michael Stewart's death in New York City, which was a sad climax of the police violence, exclusion, oppression, and exploitation that African Americans were and continue to be subjected to. Basquiat was deeply shocked by the violent death of Stewart, a graffiti artist who had been arrested while tagging a subway station. Friend and fellow New York artist Keith Haring described Basquiat as "completely freaked out … It was like it could have been him. It showed him how vulnerable he was."[30] In the aftermath, Basquiat processed the events in *The Death of Michael Stewart* (1983), which, despite the cartoon-like representation of the policemen beating the black, anonymized silhouette of Stewart, is extremely haunting. By accompanying the word "DEFACEMENT" with a "©," he grants Stewart ownership over this apparent hate crime, the police's brutal attack against him. Basquiat gifted the painting to Haring, who expressed that Old Testament–style justice, "an eye for an eye," was due.[31]

At this time, Basquiat began to work on a series of self-portraits in which he reduces himself to the same black silhouette, casting himself as the oppressed, anonymous African American, just like Stewart, a potential victim of arbitrary police mistreatment and hate crimes. The writer Glenn O'Brien shares a revealing story in this regard:

> Once, the car I was driving, with Jean-Michel as a passenger, was stopped by the police, and we had legitimate reasons to worry about being searched. I said, "They can't search us legally. They don't have probable cause." To which Jean replied, "They can do anything they want."[32]

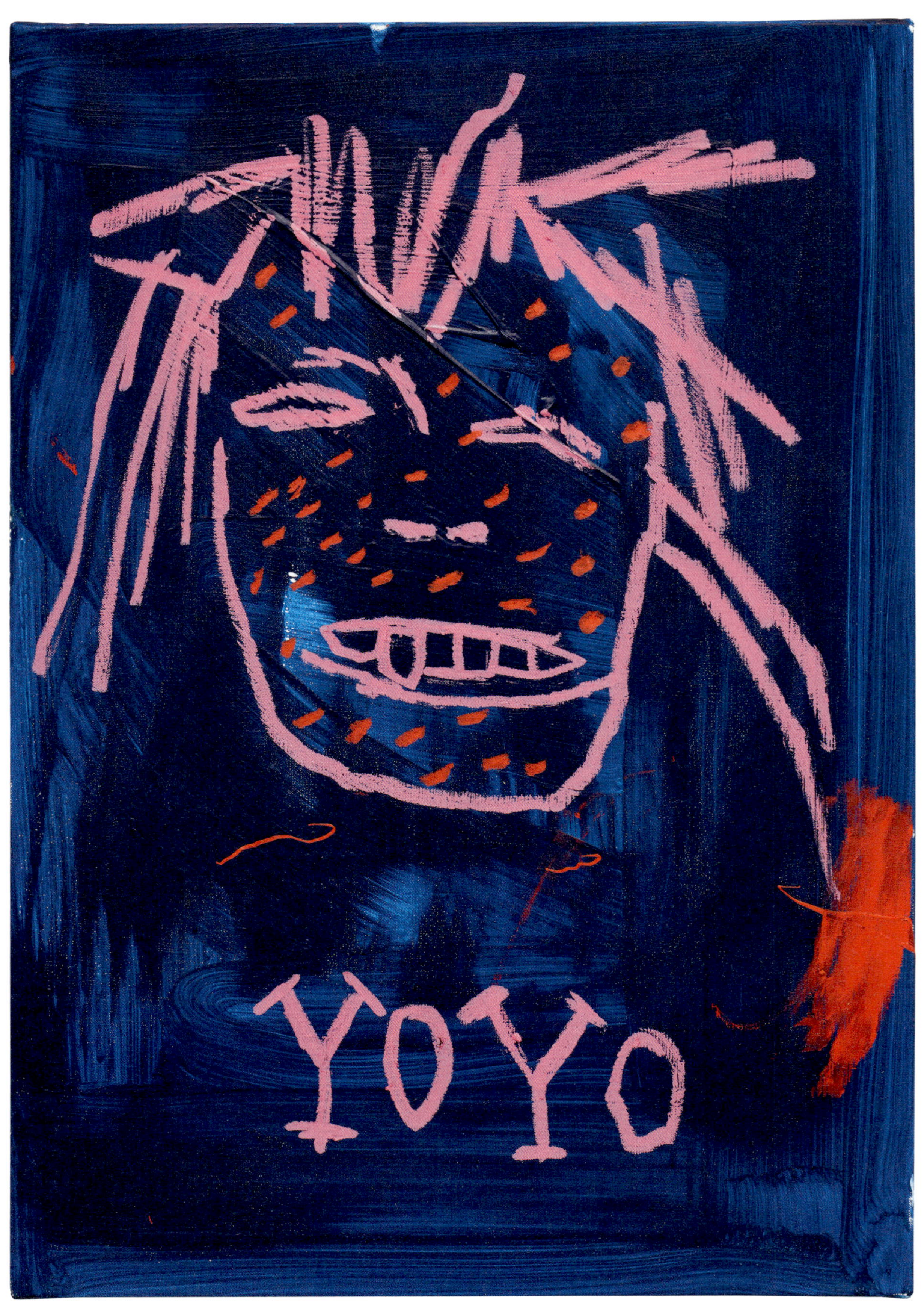

Yoyo (Portrait of Christina Bischofberger), 1983, 70.5 × 50 cm

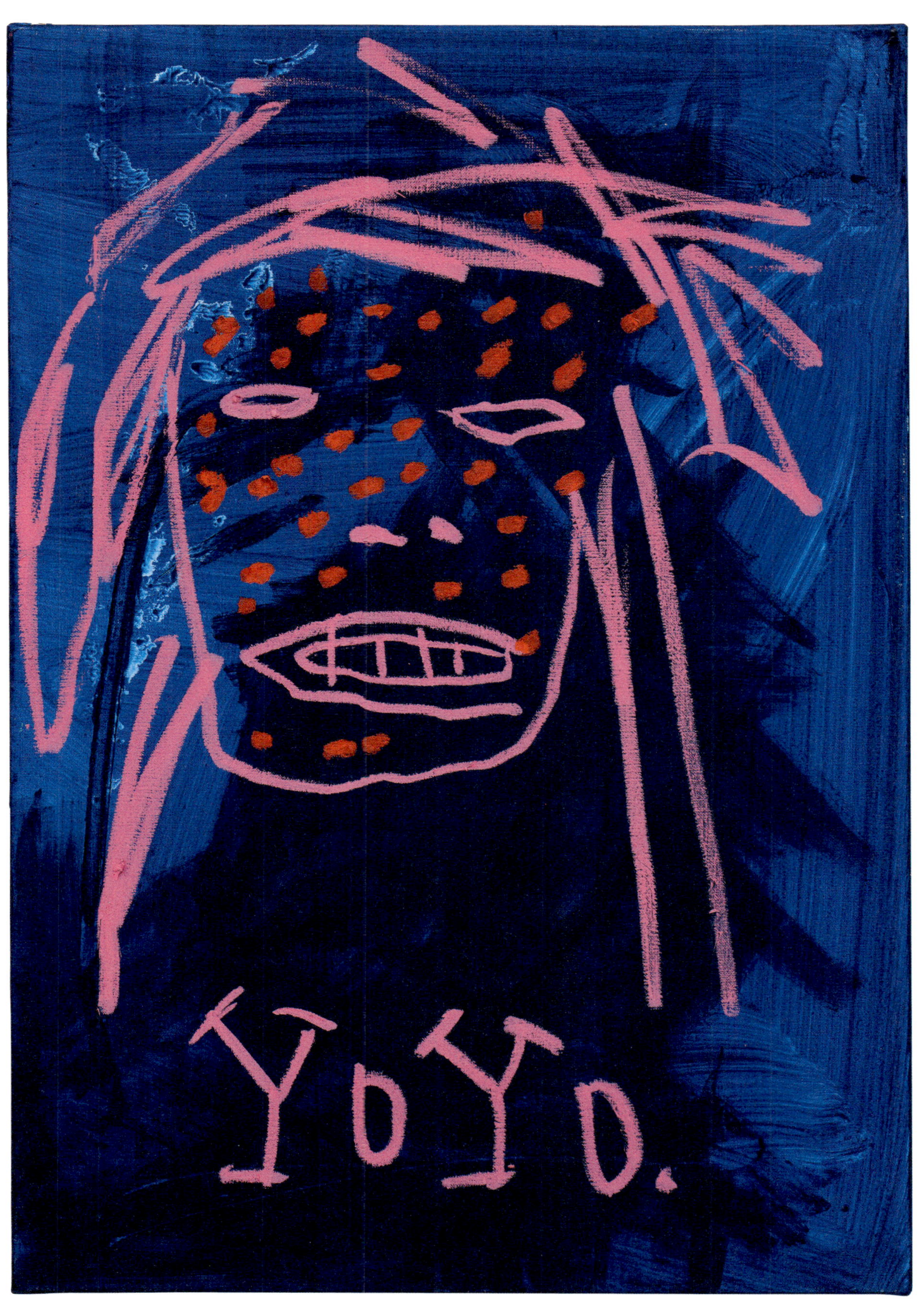

Yoyo (Portrait of Christina Bischofberger), 1983, 70.5 × 50 cm

Basquiat *was* Michael Stewart. Basquiat's works from this period show fragmented, torn figures, reflecting both their own and his own history and present. In *Punch Bag*, his apparent self-representation—with raised hands emphasized with pink paint, intense eyes, a sealed mouth, no hair, and a little internal drawing—seems arrested in movement, appearing as a silhouette-like bust, just like the other self-representations from 1983. The raised hands allude both to a gesture of defense, or "hands up," as well as the victor's pose of many of Basquiat's African American heroes—boxers. The title, *Punch Bag*, seems to suggest that the artist himself, his face, is the punch bag that the boxer will pummel, making the defensive pose and arrested movement even more strongly reflect a boxing match. At the same time, the mask-like figure becomes a powerful and totem-like figure, thus raising the question of African American identity against the backdrop of racism and oppression. Basquiat's self-questioning becomes a sign of strength and self-empowerment, making *Punch Bag*, in its apparent simplicity, a highly complex work.

The artist's return to Zurich on September 20, 1983, is recorded in the diaries of Andy Warhol, with whom Basquiat's friendship had intensified after Bischofberger's formal introduction the previous fall. Warhol writes: "Jean Michel didn't show up for the workout because he was up all night with Paige [Powell]. He's going off to Zurich. He hasn't moved into Great Jones Street yet. It was a busy afternoon."[33] Just after his arrival, Bischofberger and Basquiat drove to Appenzell, where they hiked up to "Alp Bommen just beneath the Ebenalp" so they could watch the gallerist's friend, the dairy farmer Paul Peterer, prepare his cattle for the drive downhill for the winter:

> They then followed the beautifully decorated cattle drive via Weissbad to Appenzell and further on towards Schlatt, where they were invited by Peterer to have dinner at home with him. The women were especially interested in Basquiat's dreadlocks and came to touch them. He laughed and touched their hairdos in turn.[34]

Basquiat reflected these impressions in works such as *Ski-Lift #1* (1984) and *Onion Gum* (1983), which features a skier, but they're also apparent in the inclusion of German words and sentences in other paintings, such as Untitled (Infantry) (1983). Here, Basquiat transforms all he had seen and all that had happened that year into the visual language of a cartoon, rendered life-size and set in the mental space of police violence, revolt, and war. He thus, on the one hand, breaks with tradition while, on the other, creating a new iconographic language of his and our time between Expressionism, Pop, and Conceptual Art. He transforms the injured protagonists into a comic figure with a raised bump on his head, who asks, under the "BOOM" and "BANG," in German: "WO BIN ICH?"—"WHERE AM I?"

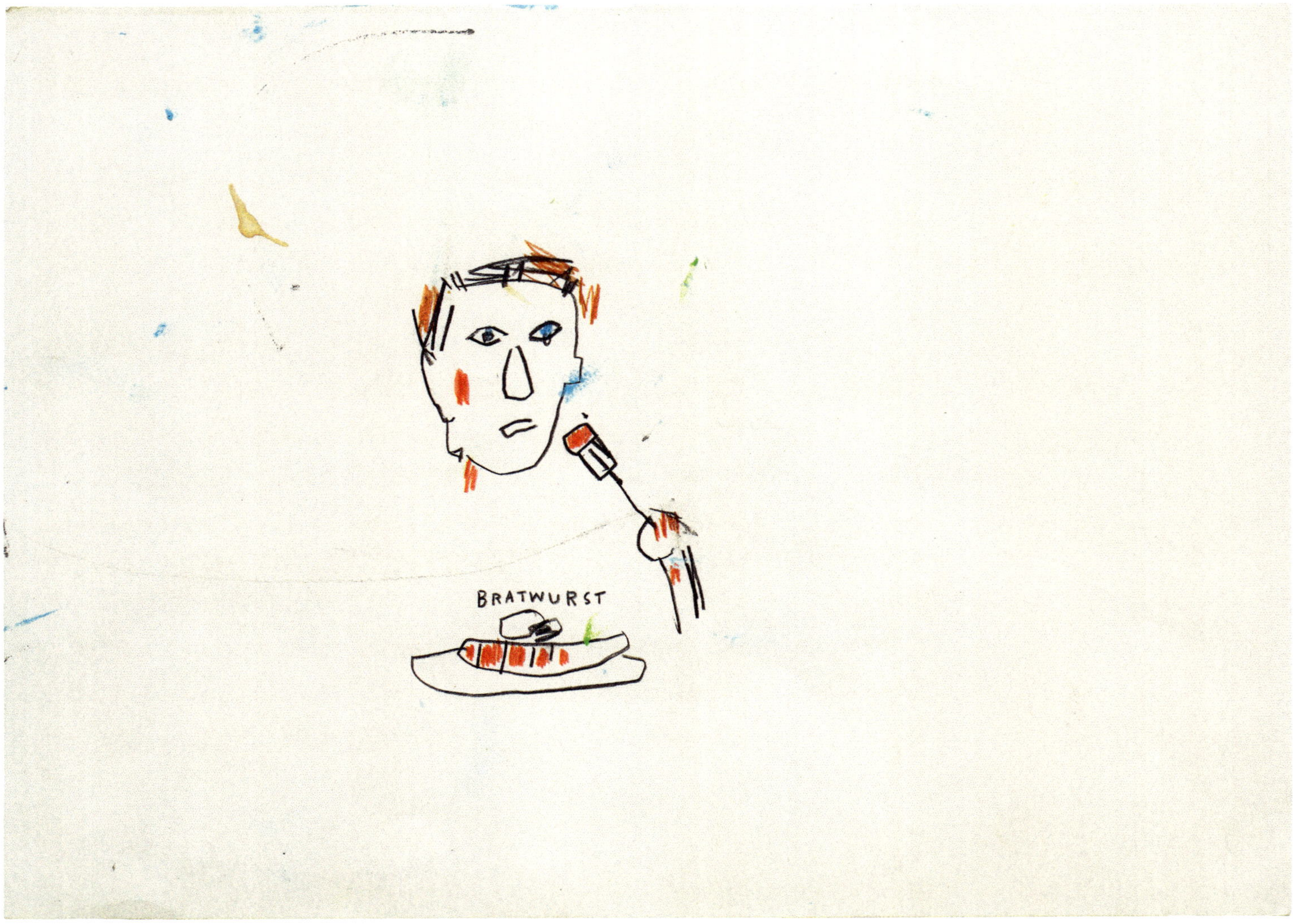

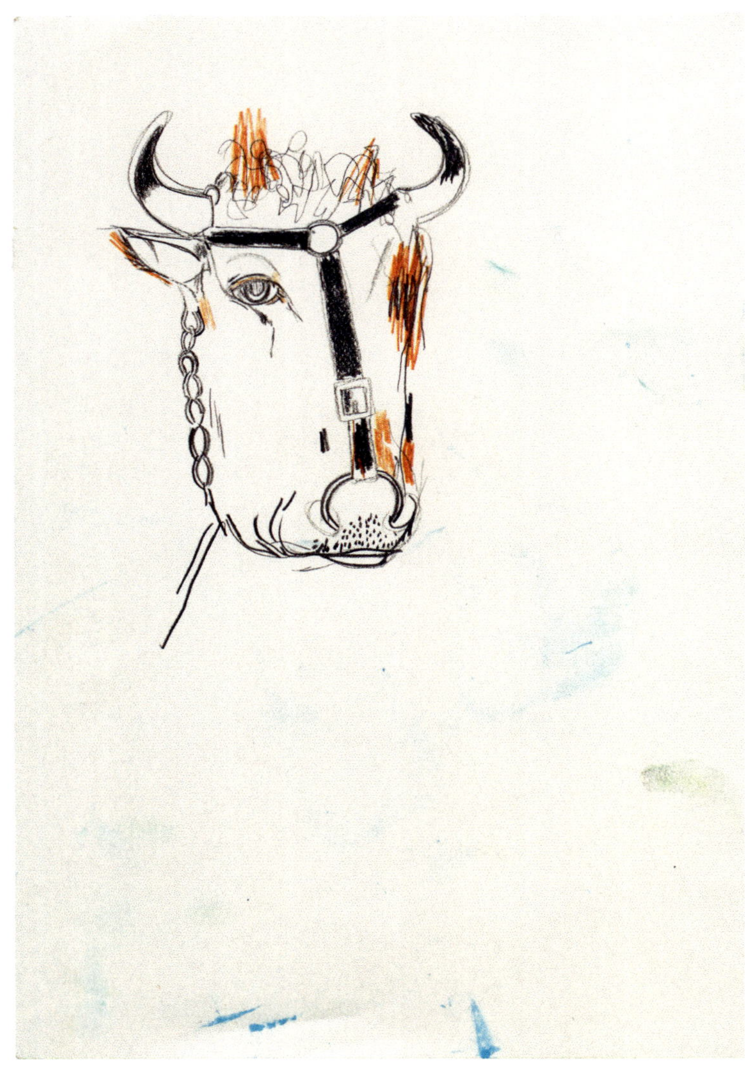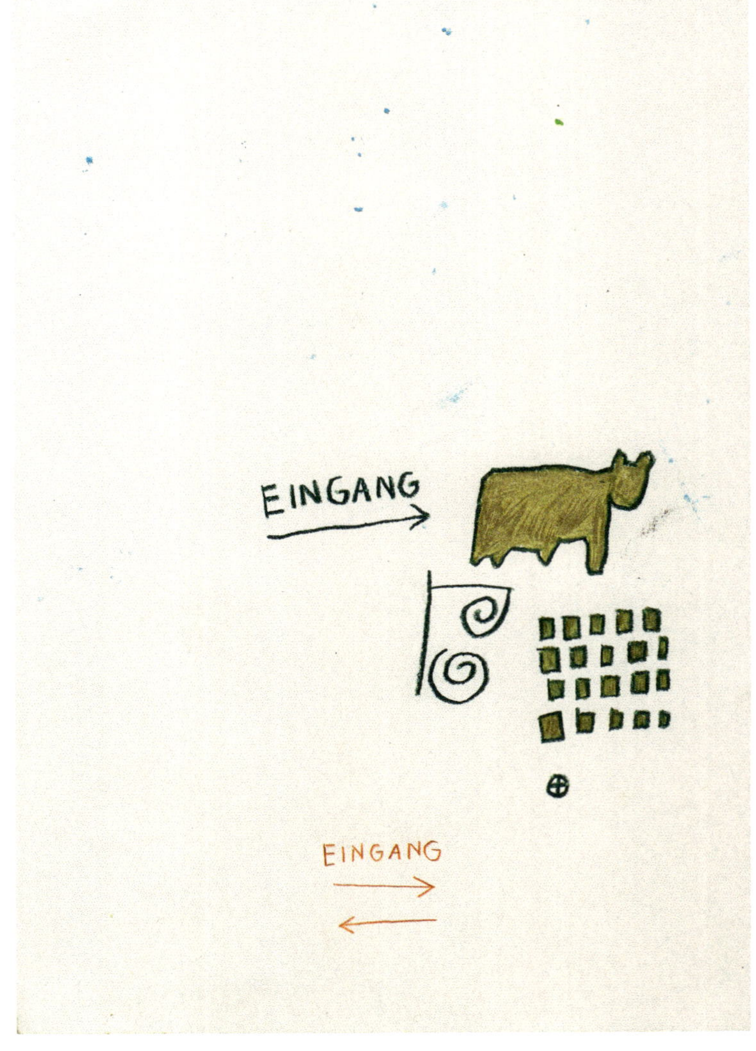

Bratwurst (Portrait of Bruno Bischofberger), 1983, 29.2 × 41.5 cm

Showbull, 1983, 41.5 × 29.2 cm

Eingang (Entrance), 1983, 41.5 × 29.2 cm

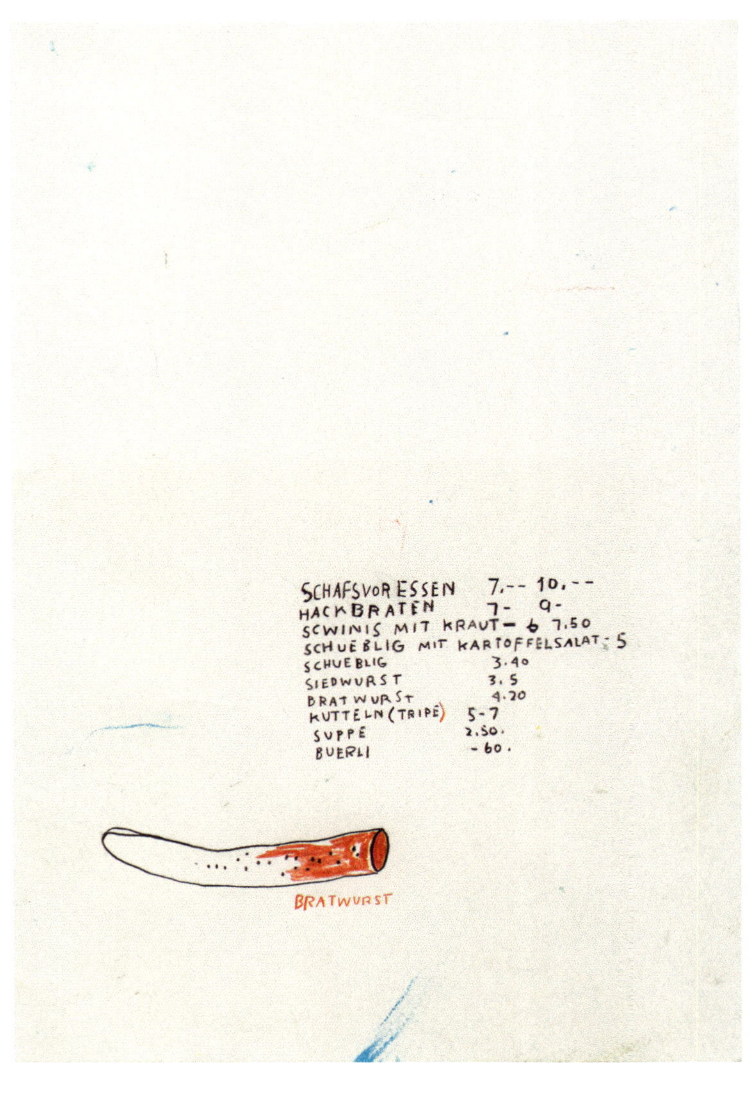

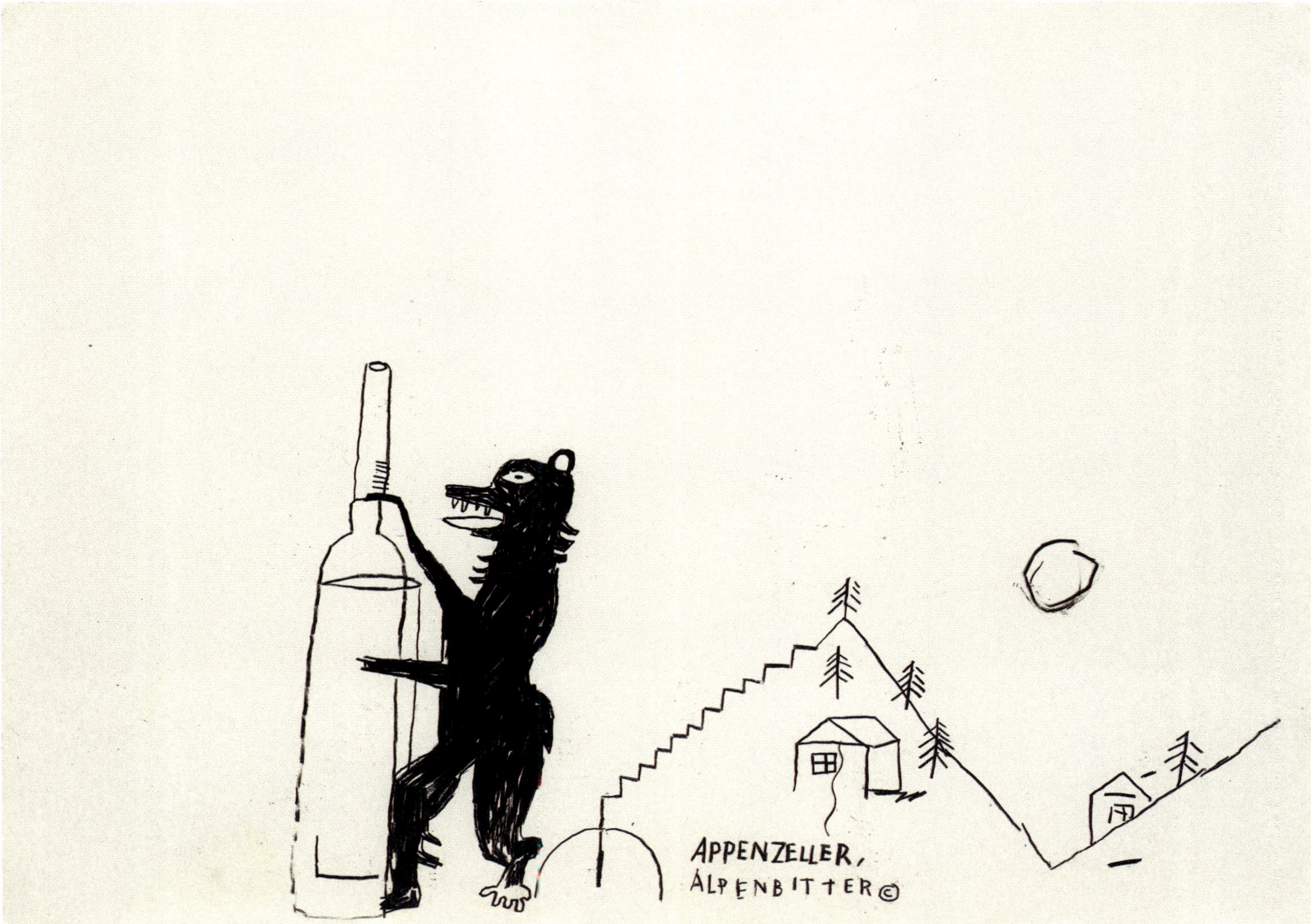

Bratwurst, 1983, 41.5 × 29.2 cm

Appenzeller Alpenbitter ©, 1983, 70 × 100 cm

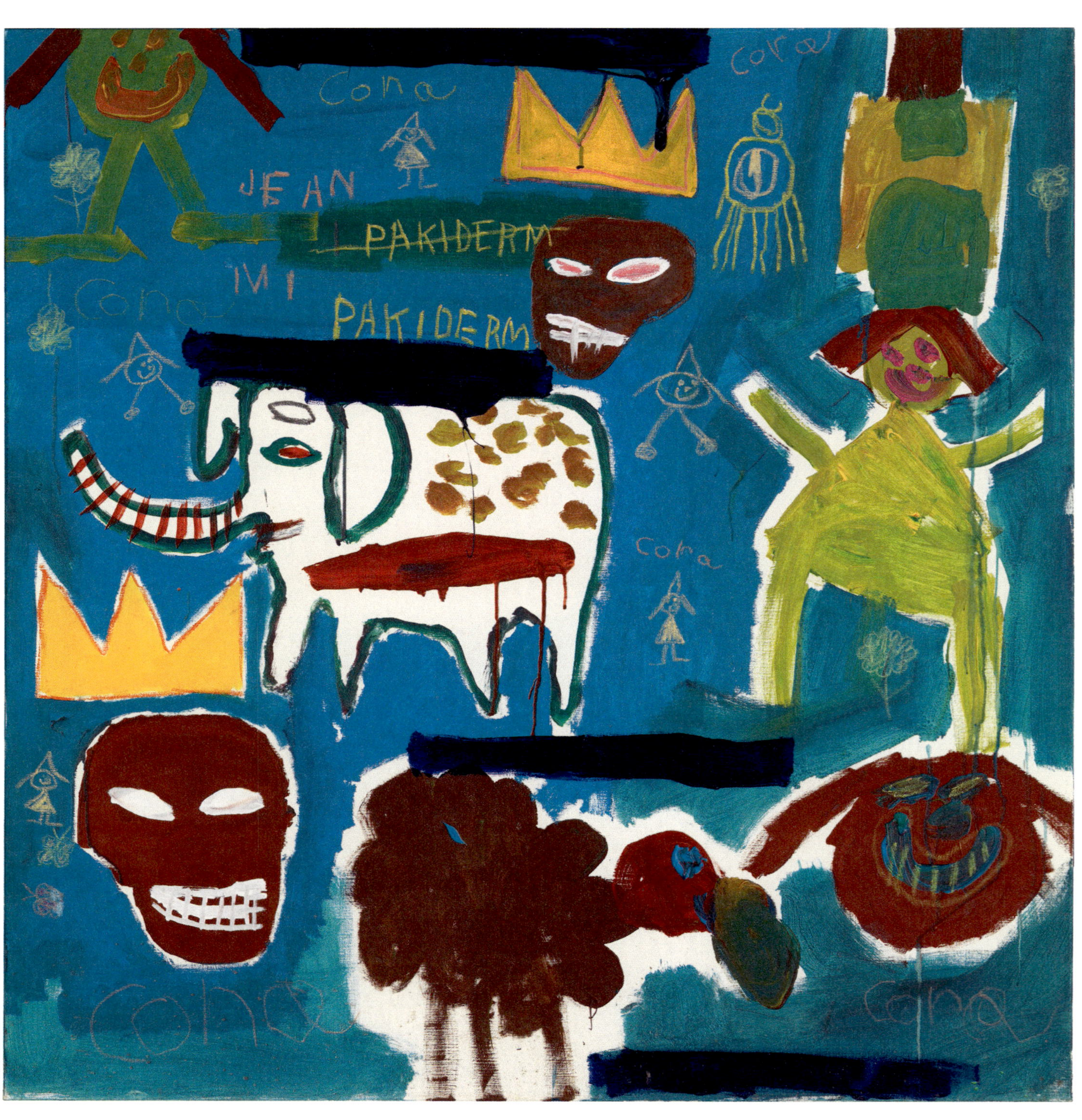

   Jean-Michel Basquiat and Cora Bischofberger, Untitled (Pakiderm), 1983, 120 × 120 cm

1983–84
The series of *cadavres exquis* by Basquiat, Warhol,
and Francesco Clemente was an initiative of
Bischofberger, who managed to convince these
three very different artist personalities he
represented to work together on a temporary
basis.[35] But the seeds of this idea came from
Basquiat's earlier collaboration with Bischofberger's
daughter, Cora, for Untitled (Pakiderm) (1983;
p. 44). Bischofberger explains:

> In the winter 1983–84, on the occasion of
> one of the many visits of Jean-Michel
> Basquiat at our home in St. Moritz, we spoke
> together about works that artists had
> done together, so called Collaborations. There
> were several reasons why we had started
> talking about them. Basquiat had done a
> 120 × 120 centimeter acrylic on canvas
> painting in our garage together with my
> daughter Cora, who was not quite four
> years old at the time. In my guest book in
> St. Moritz Basquiat drew, at the same
> time, a double page drawing [actually two],
> also with Cora. The baby-child primitive
> technique of my daughter and Basquiat's
> independently chosen "primitive" style
> were a perfect fit. Already during my first visit
> to his studio in 1982 in New York he answered
> my question about which artists had
> influenced him: "What I really like and has
> influenced me are works by three-to-
> four-year-old children." The same guest
> book shows, immediately preceding, a
> two-page colored pastel, a collaboration
> between Francesco Clemente and Cora,
> dating from the preceding winter (January
> 1983) and signed by Francesco with both
> names. Again some pages earlier, dated
> March 1982, one finds two drawings by
> Walter Dahn and Dokoupil. These artists had,
> during that stay, painted a small group
> of collaborations using acrylic on canvas
> in our garage, one of which was hanging
> in our house in the winter of 1983–84.[36]

The relevance of joint works in that contemporary moment was almost palpable.[37] The three artists seem to have begun their collaboration in early December, as Warhol's diary entry from December 20 indicates:

> Jean Michel came up to the office but he was out of it. Clemente brought up some of the paintings that the three of us are working on together, and Jean Michel was so out of it he began painting away. Jean Michel and Clemente paint each other out. There's about fifteen paintings that we're working on together.[38]

When Basquiat, Warhol, and Clemente began their joint works, three very different artists encountered one another, each already with a clearly defined profile, set of interests, and favored subject matter. Each started four paintings and one drawing, which were subsequently delivered to the other two artists, one after the other. The artists reacted to what had been drawn, painted, or silk-screened, modifying whatever was already there—like Basquiat's painted amendments of Warhol's small silkscreen paintings. Due to their highly different styles, the artists' respective contributions can be clearly distinguished from one another. Obvious differences were already apparent from the first step of preparing and priming the canvas. Warhol, for example, usually silkscreened motifs onto a white primed ground and created images characterized by flatness, whereas Clemente initiated his works with the colorful painterly priming of his practice. Basquiat, in turn, returned to his intense engagement with collaging xeroxes, which reached its first pinnacle in his production of 1983.[39]

The modifying partners likewise responded in accordingly different ways. Clemente's approach to Warhol's priming can be clearly read in *In Bianco* (In White, 1984; p. 47). Rather cautiously, he added faces. Basquiat then drew over the red one next to the middle axis with white oil stick, giving it a grimacing grin and gray hair, like Warhol's wig. Basquiat also covered most of the canvas with dark-blue paint, but left intact Warhol's silkscreen

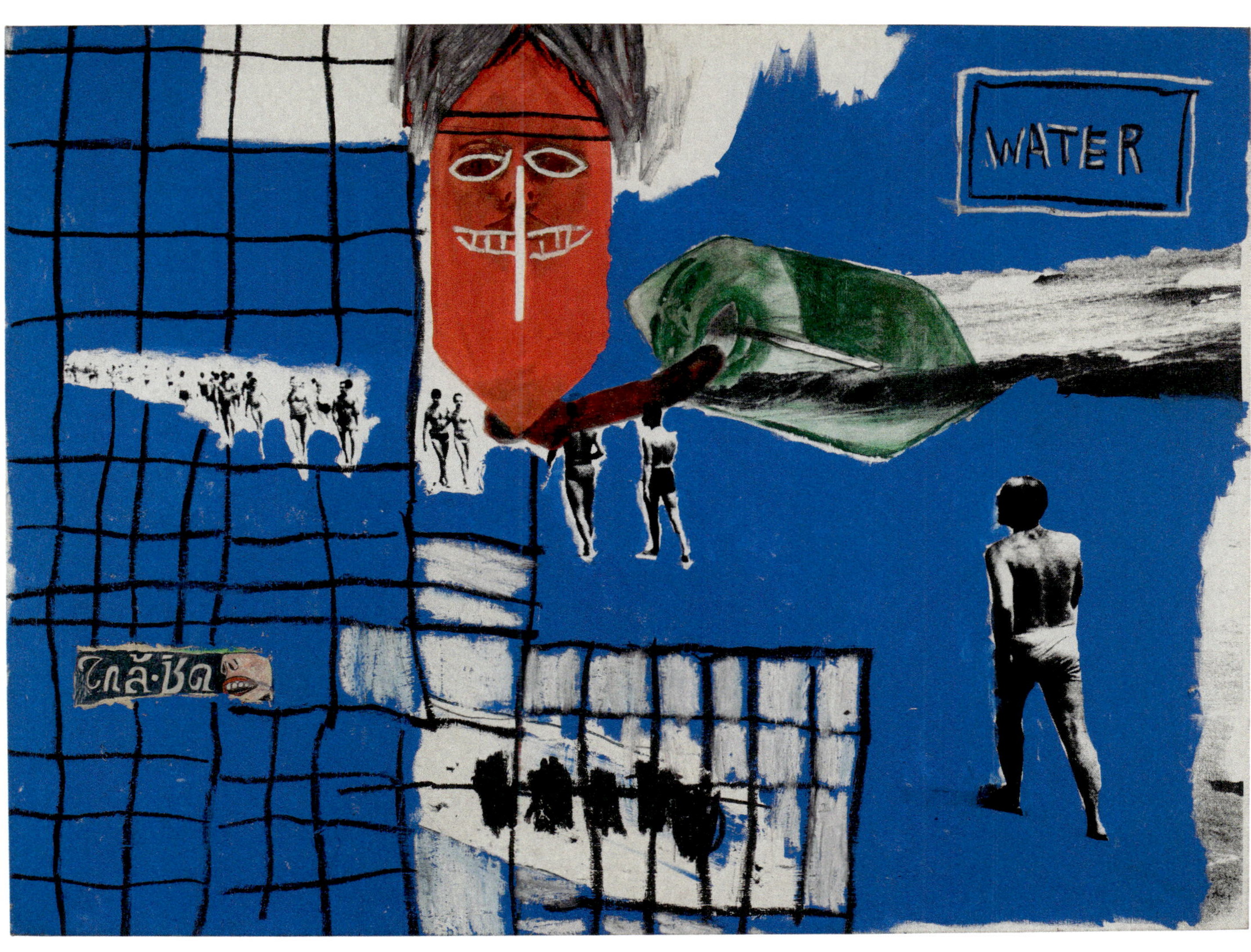

Jean-Michel Basquiat, Francesco Clemente, and Andy Warhol, *In Bianco* (In White), 1984, 122 × 168 cm

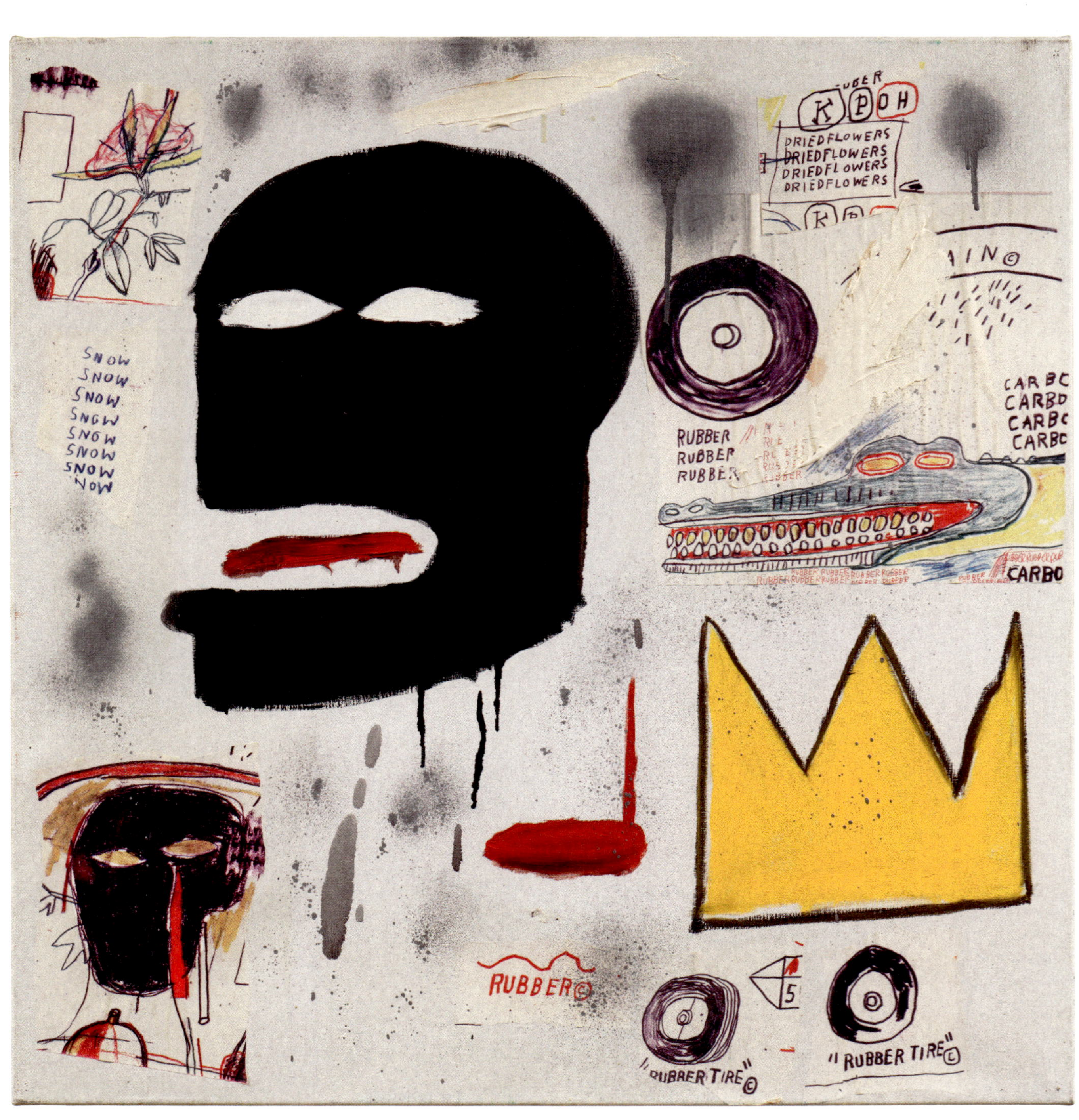

X-mas Painting for Bruno, 1984, 81 × 81 cm

of people strolling down a beach and Clemente's faces. He then added the word "WATER" to the upper right corner and placed a black grid across the painting's left half. He took up Warhol's motif of the beach and the sea, not only with the intense blue paint and the word "water," but also by leaving behind a strip of sand.

The fifteen joint works clearly show that the three artists reacted sensitively and respectfully toward the others' prior contributions, while modifying them, painting over them, or blotting them out. In contrast to the Neue Wilde artists of the late 1970s and 1980s, the trio by no means tried to approach one another stylistically, even if the "respectful approach" to the works, mentioned by Clemente and Bischofberger,[40] is legible. Bischofberger exhibited the fifteen collaborations in Zurich under the title *Collaborations: Basquiat Clemente Warhol* from September 15 to October 13, 1984. While sales were only moderately successful,[41] the cornerstone for this important collaboration was laid in St. Moritz.

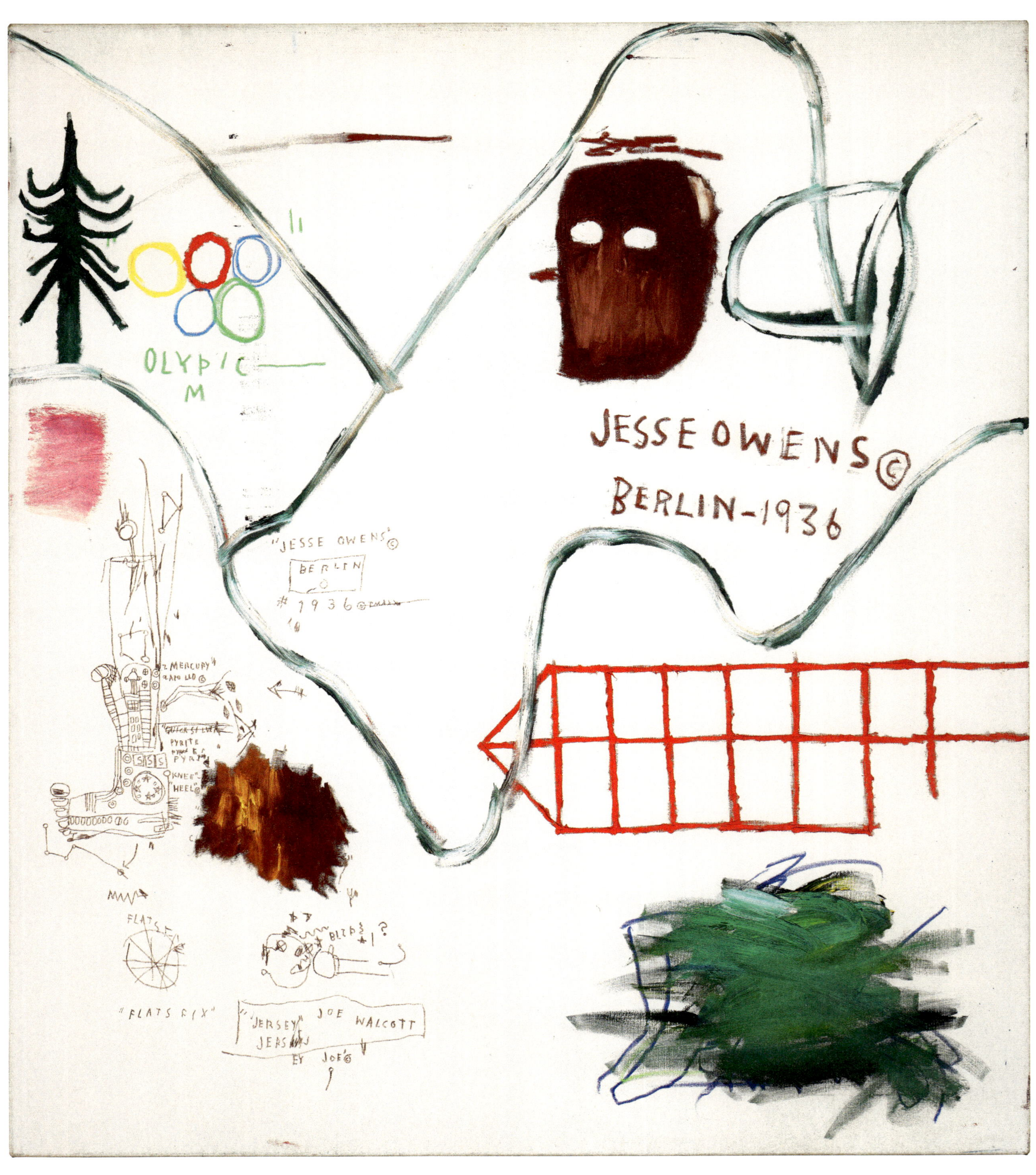

Big Snow, 1984, 168 × 151.5 cm

1984

The following year, Basquiat created a large portrait of the Bischofberger family. The gallerist recalls: "He did a big painting outside in the sunshine on the gravel in front of my house in St. Moritz of my whole family, called *The Bischofbergers* [p. 13]. There, he started off and painted until it was finished."[42] During this visit,[43] the artist also created an arresting and sanguine self-portrait (*Self-Portrait*, 1984; p. 62). The figure's eyes, nose, and ears are red, and the right eye indeed seems to be bleeding. The wide mouth, with its countless teeth, turns into an ornamental feature. The basic shades of black and brown, including the black dreadlocks, are presented in contrast to the blue-white background, which in turn is linked to the bodily presence of the artist through the scratch marks in the white paint. The bloody face here evokes the crushed skull of Michael Stewart, which the artist had depicted the year before in all its brutality in the work *In This Case* (1983).

For *Ski-Lift #1* and *Big Snow* (1984; p. 50), Basquiat once again drew on his impressions of the Engadin. In the latter, the artist links the Swiss mountains, the snow, and skiing to the 1936 Summer Olympics in Berlin, where Jesse Owens achieved a decisive victory with four gold medals, upsetting Adolf Hitler's "failed attempt to use [the Games] to prove his theories of Aryan racial superiority."[44] Owens, an African American athlete, would emerge as the most popular hero of that Olympic Games, winning his four golds for sprinting, relay, and long jump.

Meanwhile, Basquiat continued to work on his "spaces of knowledge" in St. Moritz. Bischofberger remembers how "he had books, all kinds of source material around that he used, like Gray's Anatomy. The book of hobo signs he even had in St. Moritz, when he was working in the studio there. . . . He was constantly reading something."[45]

The artist also spent Christmas with the family in St. Moritz that year. Bischofberger recalled in a conversation we had in 2024:

> The paintings that he had made [for us] in Sweden finally arrived one or two days after Christmas. Basquiat was very upset that he

had only received presents at Christmas and was unable to give any himself, so he was happy when they finally showed up. A total of twelve works arrived, and three of my four children each received a small one (about 56 by 46 cm). Since Cora painted a picture with him the year before, she was the first to select a picture, and I encouraged her to choose the nicest, maybe even the largest. My wife and I also received two larger works [including *X-mas Painting for Bruno* (1984; p. 48)]. The rest I purchased from him and several were surely left behind in Sweden.

These works are characterized by a combination of archetypal heads, usually wearing yellow crowns, which Basquiat outlined with red and black oil stick, complemented by xerox collages and spray paint, which evokes his collaborative graffiti work with Al Diaz under the name SAMO©. "I think he painted eighteen [total], all on prestretched canvases we bought at the art academy supply store," the gallerist Stellan Holm recalls. "I painted yellow on some of the crowns, but he thought I was too slow, so only on a few. These works were made in the studio of Knut Swane, a Norwegian artist who gave us the space for the night."[46] The xeroxes repeat the words "RUBBER," "CARBON," and "DRIED FLOWERS" and one includes the head of an alligator.

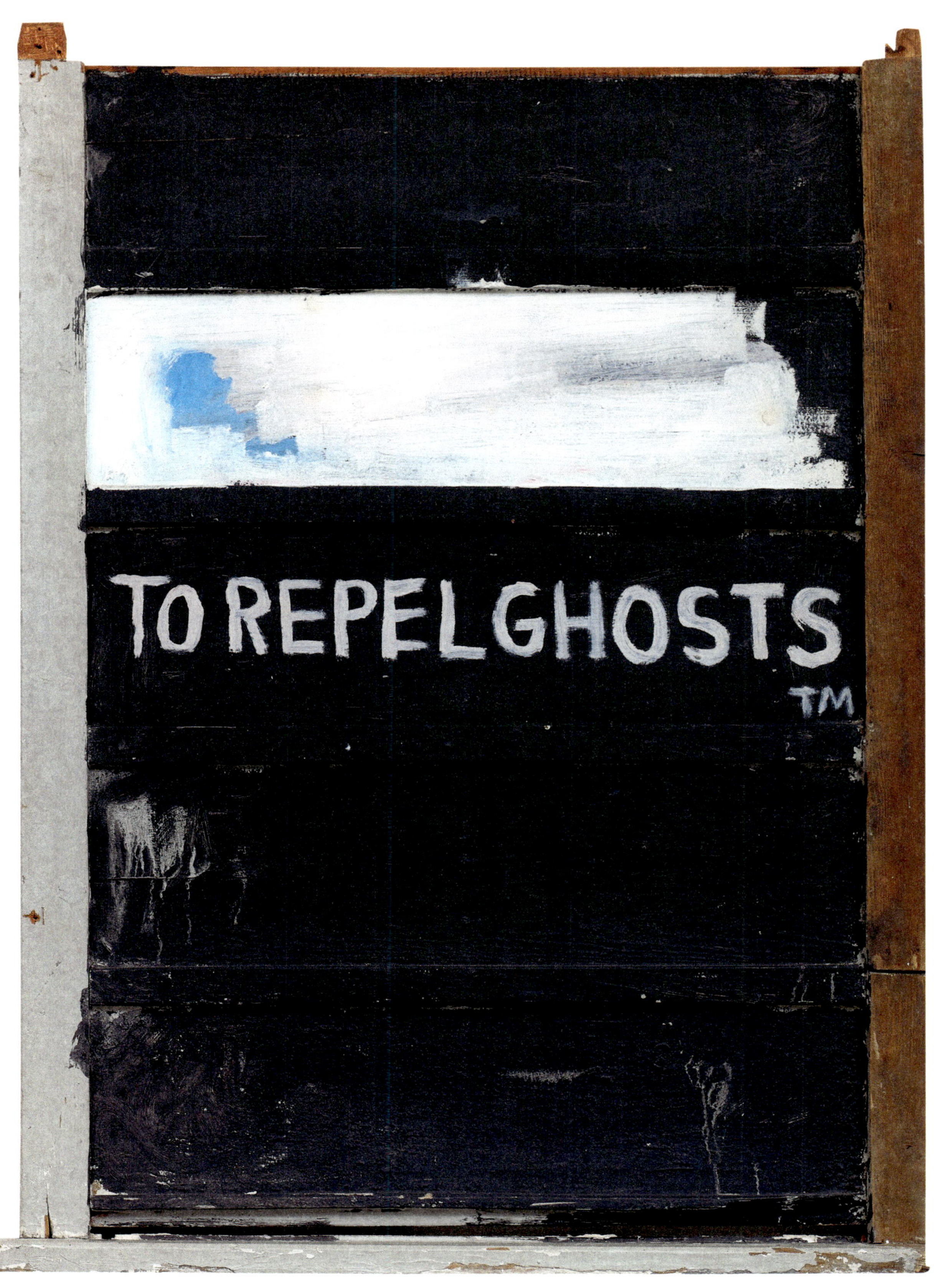

To Repel Ghosts, 1986, 112 × 83 × 10 cm

1985
Basquiat's third solo show at Galerie Bruno Bischofberger was held from January 19 to February 16,
1985, under the title *Jean-Michel Basquiat: New
Works*.[47] The artist was also included in the
group exhibition *The Engadine in Painting* at the
Segantini Museum in St. Moritz, where he showed
the work *See*. It remains unclear which works
Basquiat created in the summer of 1985 during his
stay in St. Moritz, however. As journalist Phoebe
Hoban recounts in her biography of Basquiat:

> The artist was painting in Bischofberger's
> studio/chalet, when he got a call from Leonart
> DeKnegt, a self-described "gallery brat"
> and former assistant, who had worked with
> him in both New York and Los Angeles. . . .
> Now he decided to join Basquiat in Switzer-
> land. When DeKnegt arrived at the Palace
> Hotel, where Basquiat was staying, the two
> immediately went off on a shopping spree.
> "We bought like thousands upon thousands
> of dollars of clothes and shoes," recalls
> DeKnegt. "I remember we were getting
> dressed, and had just ordered this super
> expensive breakfast, when we got a call
> from Bruno that he was downstairs with
> a couple of clients. So we went and started
> talking with them about Italian painters,
> and all of a sudden, we decided to go to
> Florence."[48]

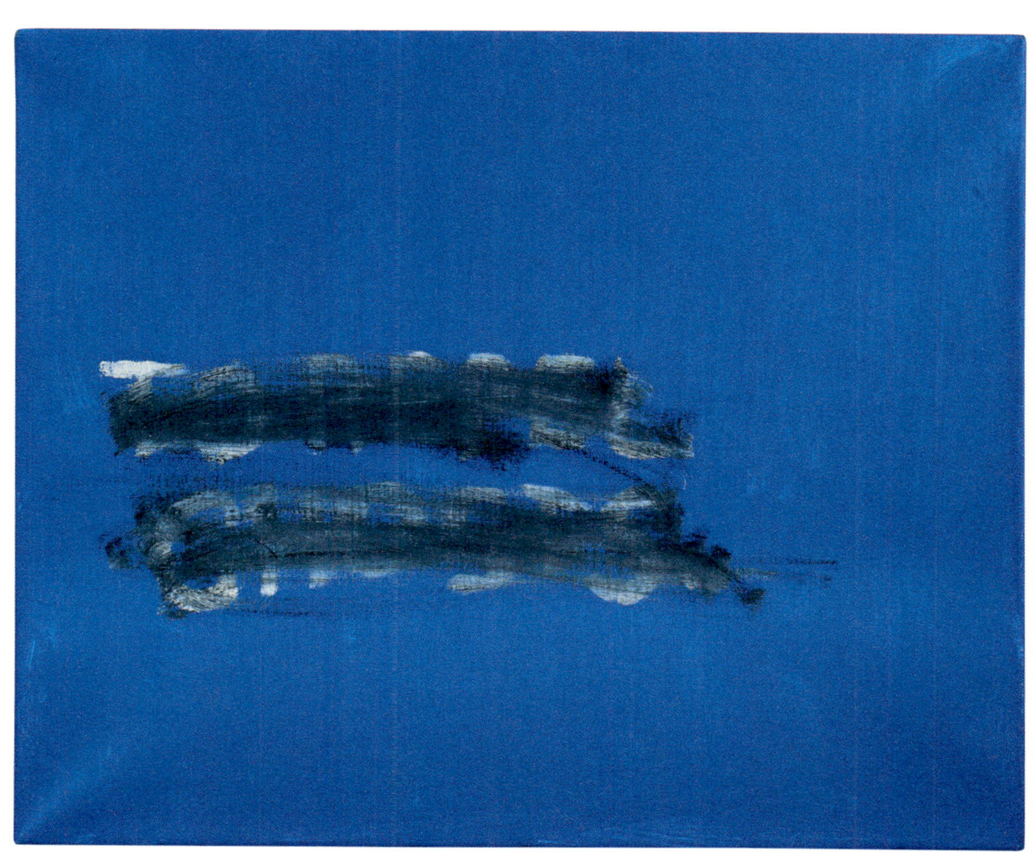

To Repel Ghosts, 1986, 35.6 × 41.2 cm

To Repel Ghosts, 1986, 30.5 × 50.2 cm

1986
The years 1986 to 1988 in Basquiat's life are clearly
marked by an alternation between the void
and a fear of the void. From April 26 to June 30,
Bischofberger presented Basquiat's fourth
solo show at the gallery, focused on drawings,[49]
and in November, an exhibition of collaborations
between Warhol and Basquiat followed.[50]

In 1986, while in Switzerland, Basquiat created
a group of works based on the phrase "to repel
ghosts" (pp. 53, 55–56). As in the "hunting-lodge"
paintings, the artist works with a foundation of one
color. In two of them, "TO REPEL GHOSTS" appears
in white paint on a blue backdrop, which the artist
then crossed out with black acrylic—deleting while
emphasizing the words by doing so. On one of
these canvases the phrase appears on a single line,
while on the other the words stack on top of each
other. Basquiat had returned to the idea of "to repel
ghosts"—which he had already used as the title
for a portrait of his friend, the artist Jack Walls, in the
spring—due to a conversation about his upcoming
exhibition in Abidjan. As Bischofberger explains:

> When we went [to S-chanf in the Engadin]
> to visit this friend of mine, Claudio
> Caratsch, who was the Swiss ambassador
> in Africa for four countries with a seat in
> Abidjan on the Ivory Coast, he told Basquiat,
> "You know, in Africa art is made in a
> different way. Here it is art for art's sake,
> and in Africa art is only made in order
> to do something with it, 'to repel ghosts,'
> for instance." Basquiat didn't say anything,
> but when we drove home Basquiat said
> to me, he knew of course about repelling
> ghosts, but he didn't want to offend him
> [the ambassador] so he didn't say anything.
> He was quite amused that the ambassador,
> a studied ethnographer, was telling him
> about things he already knew. Right after, back
> in St. Moritz, he wrote "to repel ghosts" on
> two little paintings. The next week in Zurich
> he painted a bigger work "to repel ghosts"
> on [a] piece of wood which was broken off in
> an old storage of my gallery, when it was
> standing there to be transported away.[51]

It seems as if Basquiat transferred these words, which speak of and to the world of spirits and the transition from life to death, like an incantation to the canvas. The *To Repel Ghosts* works are consciously spiritual and act like altarpieces or magical objects with totemistic powers for the beholder. The paintings' inherent duality lies in the tension between the combination of image and object, their symbolic significance, and the practical power of an exorcism.[52] Alongside the two blue canvas works described above, Basquiat also declared "TO REPEL GHOSTS" on a wooden panel. This time, the phrase is written with no space between the words, followed by a trademark symbol. Unlike on the canvases, the words are clearly legible, painted in white on a black background. A thick white bar appears above them, almost the same length as the phrase, with a patch of blue on the left side. Here, Basquiat mixes both the materiality and the spirituality of *nkisi* power figures with those of Western culture, as well as "a symbol of power in many African visual traditions."[53]

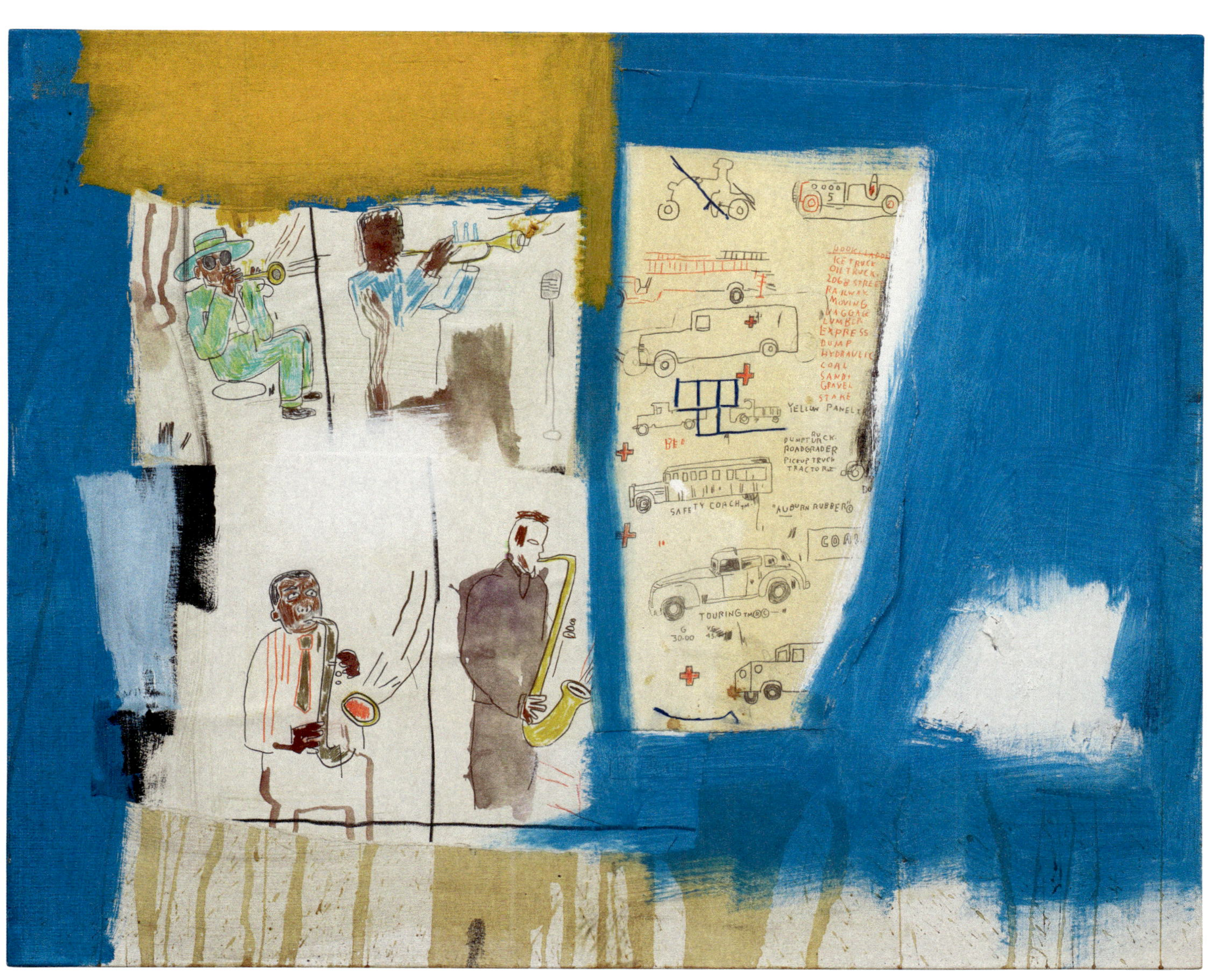

Worthy Constituents, 1986, 70 × 90 cm

Not all the works that Basquiat created in St. Moritz and elsewhere in Switzerland can be identified without a doubt. But we know they include various artistic subjects that combine life in the metropolis of New York, the lived experience of racism, and the culture of the African diaspora with the influence of the cultural and natural landscape of the Engadin. Basquiat also continued to use the German language in his drawings, such as Untitled (Achtung) from 1987. According to Bischofberger, who spent so much time living and working alongside the artist, Basquiat also created etchings and lithographs while in Switzerland:

> I do not know exactly, but he was interested in every technique. He also did monoprints [actually etchings]. … He did only five or six monoprints … [he] was very proud of them. He showed them to me and asked, "Do you want to buy them?" They did cost at least as much as a drawing, even more, and so I took the one I liked best. I still have that. Basquiat also did [several] lithographs. He sat down here in Switzerland and worked [Bischofberger had arranged that Basquiat could work with a lithographer in St. Gallen]. He gave me a couple of proof prints.[54]

When we explore Basquiat's time in Switzerland, it soon becomes clear that the artist was unable to withdraw from the "revelation of beauty" through which the "riddles of existence" are forgotten[55]—the mountains, the ibexes, the ski lifts, the bratwursts, and the hospitality of the Bischofberger family. Bruno Bischofberger also remembers this time as one of joy and discovery:

> Having been Jean-Michel's main art dealer for the greatest part of his short life as an artist brought me, and also my family, into a close friendship with him which is reflected in his many visits to Switzerland: Zurich, Appenzell and St. Moritz; and in our joint travels to Scotland, Italy, Spain and the Ivory Coast.[56]

For Basquiat, the Engadin meant work, inspiration, friendship, and rest and relaxation, all at the same time.

1 Sten Nadolny, *The Discovery of Slowness,* trans. Ralph Freedman (Edinburgh: Canongate, 2003), 107–8.
2 Jakob Christoph Heer, *Streifzüge im Engadin* (Frauenfeld, Switzerland: Huber, 1898), 48.
3 Conrad Ferdinand Meyer, quoted in Jörg Huber, "The Dream of the Roof: The Interaction between Landscape and Painting," *Das Oberengadin in der Malerei / L 'Engadina alta nella pittura / The Engadine in Painting*, trans. Judith Ditzel et al. (St. Moritz, Switzerland: Verkehrsverein Oberengadin, 1985), 42.
4 Ewa Hess, "Galerist Bruno Bischofberger erinnert sich," *Ewa Hess Feuilleton* (blog), May 2, 2010, http://www.ewahess.ch/bruno-bischofberger-erinnert-sich/.
5 Michel Nuridsany, *Jean-Michel Basquiat* (Paris: Flammarion, 2015), 278.
6 Carlo McCormick, "Tony Shafrazi with Carlo McCormick," in *Basquiat x Warhol: Painting Four Hands* (Paris: Éditions Gallimard, 2023), 297.
7 Roland Barthes, "Cy Twombly: Works on Paper," in *The Responsibility of Forms: Critical Essays on Music, Art, and Representation*, trans. Richard Howard (New York: Farrar, Straus and Giroux, 1985), 170.
8 See Dieter Buchhart, "Egon Schiele – Cy Twombly – Jean-Michel Basquiat: It's All Drawing and the Emancipation of Dissonance," trans. Brian Currid, in *Poetics of the Gesture: Schiele, Twombly, Basquiat*, ed. Dieter Buchhart (New York: Nahmad Contemporary, 2014), 14–27.
9 Buchhart, "It's All Drawing."
10 See Nadolny, *The Discovery of Slowness.*
11 R. Staub, quoted in Eduard Campbell, "The Most Unique Mountainous Region in the World: The Engadine from the Ice Age to Colonization," in *The Engadine in Painting*, 20.
12 Suzanne Mallouk, quoted in Jennifer Clement, *Widow Basquiat: A Love Story* (Edinburgh: Canongate, 2000), 73–74.
13 Storr coined the term "eye rap" specifically in reference to Basquiat's inimitable visual rhythm. Robert Storr, "Two Hundred Beats per Min.," in *Jean-Michel Basquiat: Drawings*, ed. John Cheim (New York: Robert Miller Gallery, 1990), unpaginated.
14 According to Senegalese historian Cheikh Anta Diop, the Nubians are the ancestors of almost all Africans. Nubian culture is considered the start of African civilization. Lower Nubia was one of the first developed states and already existed before ancient Egypt. See Cheikh Anta Diop, *The African Origin of Civilization: Myth or Reality* (New York: Lawrence Hill Books, 1974), 150.
15 See Lerone Bennett Jr., *Before the Mayflower: A History of Black America* (New York: Penguin, 1988).
16 Keith Haring, "Remembering Basquiat: Keith Haring on a Fellow Artist and a Friend," in *Jean-Michel Basquiat* (New York: Tony Shafrazi Gallery, 1999), 24.

17 Samuel Beckett, "The Unnamable," in *Three Novels* (New York: Grove, 2009), 413.
18 Bruno Bischofberger, "Knowing Basquiat," in *The Jean-Michel Basquiat Reader*, ed. Jordana Moore Saggese (Oakland: University of California Press, 2021), 166.
19 Hess, "Galerist Bruno Bischofberger erinnert sich."
20 Nuridsany, *Jean-Michel Basquiat*, 275. See also Phoebe Hoban, *Basquiat: A Quick Killing in Art* (New York: Viking Penguin, 1998), 134–35.
21 Nuridsany, *Basquiat*, 275 and Hoban, *Basquiat,* 134–35.
22 Jean-Michel Basquiat, quoted in Robert Farris Thompson, "Royalty, Heroism, and the Streets: The Art of Jean-Michel Basquiat," in *Jean-Michel Basquiat*, ed. Richard Marshall, (New York: Harry N. Abrams, 1992), 32.
23 My thanks to Bruno Bischofberger for our extensive conversations since 2009, most recently on September 12, 2024.
24 See https://www.brunobischofberger.com/basquiat-biography.
25 Siegfried Gohr, *Expressive Malerei nach Picasso* (Basel: Galerie Beyeler, 1983). See Anna Karina Hofbauer, "Chronology," in *Jean-Michel Basquiat* (Paris: Éditions Gallimard, 2018), 315.
26 Private conversation with Bruno Bischofberger, conversation with the author.
27 Hess, "Galerist Bruno Bischofberger erinnert sich."
28 Jon Bollmann, "Könige, Heldentum und die Strasse," *Transhelvetica: Die Kunst des Reisens* 64 (April–May 2021): 56–57.
29 Bollmann, "Könige, Heldentum und die Strasse," 56–57.
30 Keith Haring, quoted in Anthony Haden-Guest, "Burning Out," *Vanity Fair.* November 1988, 190.
31 Keith Haring, journal entry, March 28, 1987, in *Keith Haring: Journals* (New York: Penguin Books, 2010), 166.
32 Glenn O'Brien, "Basquiat and the New York Scene 1978–82," in *Basquiat*, ed. Dieter Buchhart (Ostfildern, Germany: Hatje Cantz Verlag, 2010), viii.
33 Andy Warhol, diary entry, September 20, 1983, in *The Andy Warhol Diaries*, ed. Pat Hackett (New York: Warner, 1989), 528.
34 Bollmann, "Könige, Heldentum und die Strasse," 56. See also Hess, "Galerist Bruno Bischofberger erinnert sich."
35 Bruno Bischofberger, "Collaborations: Betrachtungen und Erfahrungen mit Basquiat, Clemente, Warhol," in *Collaborations: Warhol, Basquiat, Clemente*, ed. Tilman Osterwold (Ostfildern-Ruit, Germany: Cantz, 1996), 108.
36 See https://www.brunobischofberger.com/collabs-origin.
37 Wolfgang Max Faust, "Gemeinschaftsbilder. Ein Aspekt der neuen Malerei," *Kunstforum International*, November 1983, https://www.kunstforum.de/band/1983-67-zwischenbilanz-1-gemeinschaftsbilder/.

38 Andy Warhol, diary entry, December 20, 1983, in *The Andy Warhol Diaries*, 545.
39 Dieter Buchhart, "It's All Xerox: Jean-Michel Basquiat's Spaces of Knowledge Yesterday, Today, and Tomorrow," trans. Brian Currid, in *Jean-Michel Basquiat: Xerox* (New York: Nahmad Contemporary, 2019).
40 Bruno Bischofberger, conversation with the author, March 17, 2011, and Francesco Clemente, conversation with the author, May 2, 2011.
41 Bruno Bischofberger, "Bruno Bischofberger im Gespräch mit Dieter Buchhart, März 2011," *Ménage à trois*: Warhol, Basquiat, Clemente (Bielefeld, Germany: Kerber, 2012), 45. Warhol made a critical note on the lack of sales: "These combined paintings of Jean Michel and me and Clemente that he said were 'just a curiosity that nobody would want to buy' that he paid $20,000 for like fifteen pictures for, he's now selling for $40,000 or $60,000 a piece! Yes! And I have a funny feeling that he's actually giving Clemente more because I can't see him doing this for this little. And I should get more because I bring up the prices . . . oh but well, Jean Michel got me into painting differently. so that's a good thing" (Andy Warhol, diary entry, September 17, 1984, in *The Andy Warhol Diaries*, 600).
42 Bischofberger, "Knowing Basquiat," 167.
43 A handwritten note by Bruno Bischofberger on the rear of a reproduction of the work from February 27, 1994.
44 "Olympic Games Berlin 1936," Olympic Games, n.d., https://olympics.com/en/olympic-games/berlin-1936.
45 Bischofberger, "Knowing Basquiat," 168.
46 Stellan Holm, conversation with the author, September 20, 2024.
47 See https://www.brunobischofberger.com/basquiat-biography. See also Larry Warsh, ed., *Basquiat-isms* (Princeton, IL: Princeton University Press, 2019), 107.
48 Hoban, *Basquiat: A Quick Killing in Art*, 260.
49 See https://www.brunobischofberger.com/basquiat-biography.
50 See https://www.brunobischofberger.com/basquiat-biography.
51 Bischofberger, "Knowing Basquiat," 168.
52 See Joshua White, "Jean-Michel Basquiat in the Nicola Erni Collection," in *Jean-Michel Basquiat*, ed. Nicola Erni (Steinhausen, Switzerland: Nicola Erni Collection, 2018), 25.
53 Aleesa Alexander, "Homage to Malcolm," in *Odyssey: Jack Whitten. Sculpture, 1963–2017*, ed. Katy Siegel (New York: Gregory R. Miller, 2018), 45–46.
54 Bischofberger, "Knowing Basquiat," 169–70.
55 Meyer, quoted in Huber, "The Dream of the Roof," 42.
56 Bruno Bischofberger, preface to *Basquiat* (Milan: Edizioni Charta, 1999), 13.

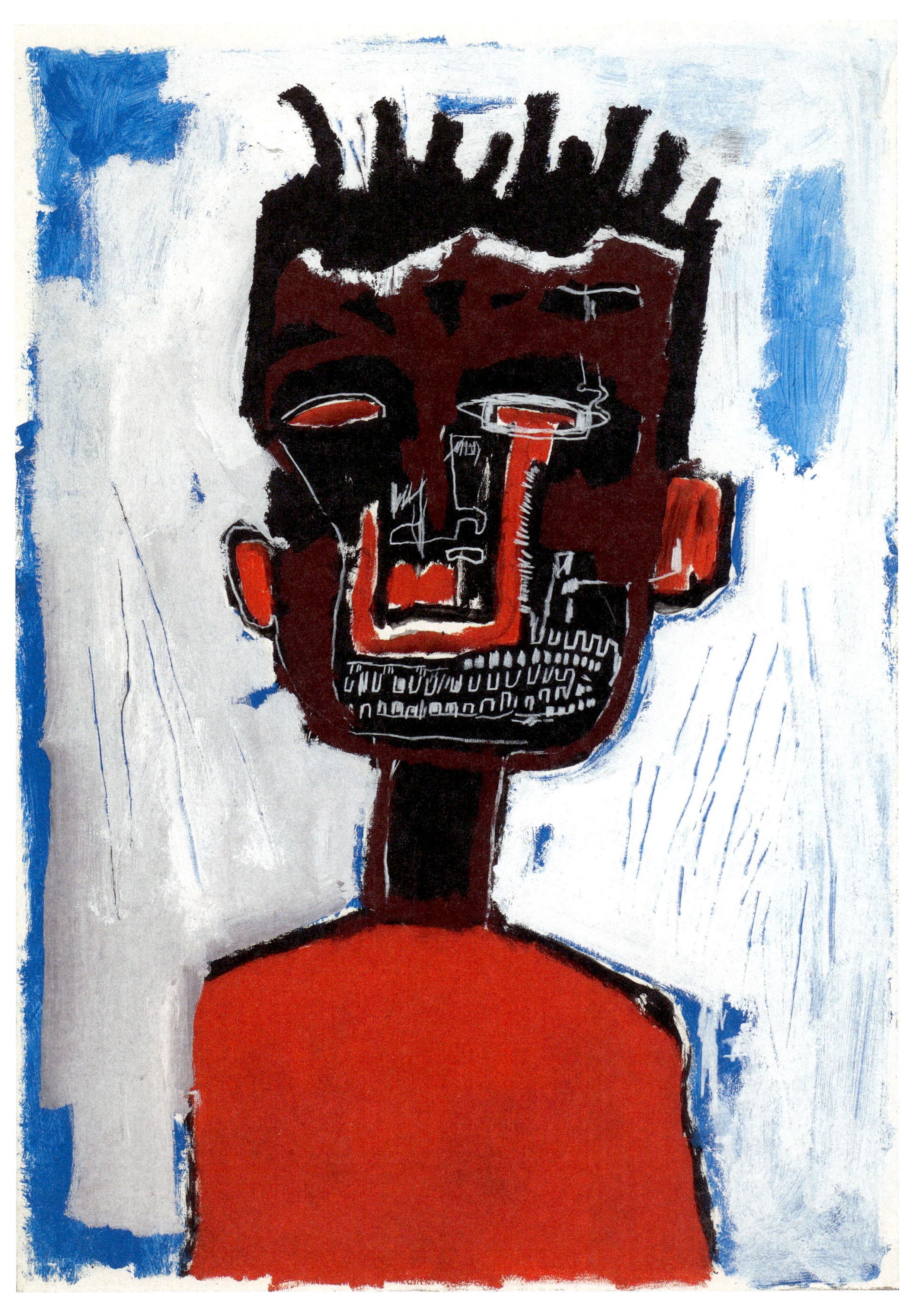

Self-Portrait, 1984, 100 × 70 cm

Jean-Michel Basquiat

Jean-Michel Basquiat (1960–1988) began his artistic career covering the walls of Downtown New York with conceptual, poetic graffiti. His symbol-laden artworks address political issues, criticizing racism, social injustices, and consumer capitalism. With their skeleton-like silhouettes, mask-like grimaces, and pictograms, his paintings combine the explosive visual codes of the streets of New York with the cultural heritage of humankind, blurring the line between imagery, words, and signs.

Defying the prevailing Conceptual and Minimal art of the time, Basquiat established a new figurative and expressive language inspired by everyday life and popular culture as well as African spiritual objects. The intensity and energy of his idiosyncratic work sent shock waves through society. In 1982, he was the youngest artist ever to participate in the renowned international art exhibition Documenta, and he continues to have a major influence on contemporary art.

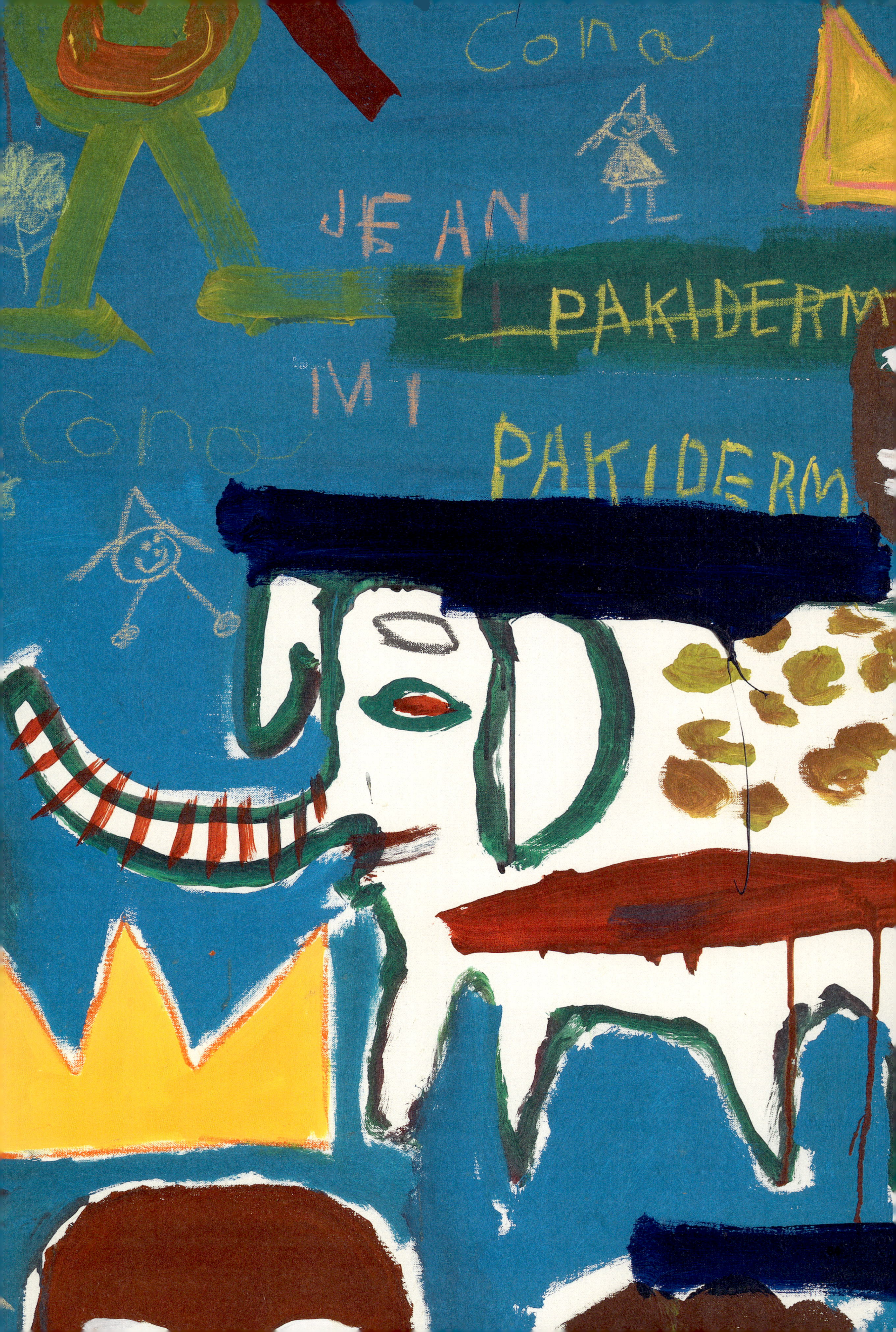

cona
JEAN
PAKIDERM
IMI
cona
PAKIDERM

Chronology

This chronology is based on various sources, particularly the biographies *Jean-Michel Basquiat* by Michel Nuridsany and *Basquiat: A Quick Killing in Art* by Phoebe Hoban, as well as interviews with Bruno Bischofberger, especially those collected in *The Jean-Michel Basquiat Reader* by Jordana Moore Saggese. The Basquiat biography on Galerie Bruno Bischofberger's website was extremely helpful too.

1981

Spring
A few days after curator Diego Cortez first showed works by Jean-Michel Basquiat to Bruno Bischofberger in Cortez's iconic *New York/New Wave* exhibition, Bischofberger visits the Annina Nosei Gallery to view a piece by Francesco Clemente. That same year, Nosei had become Basquiat's first gallerist. In the basement of her gallery, which Basquiat is using as a studio, Bischofberger observes the painter at work. Their more momentous first personal meeting, however, takes place a few months later.

1982

May
Bischofberger learns from his assistant in New York that Basquiat has left Nosei's gallery due to professional differences. A little later, during a visit to the artist's new studio on Crosby Street in Manhattan, Bischofberger offers to represent him. They agree that Bischofberger will be Basquiat's exclusive dealer worldwide—an agreement that will hold until the artist's death.

September
After Bischofberger becomes Basquiat's gallerist, the two plan an exhibition at Galerie Bruno Bischofberger in Zurich for early fall of that same year. From September 11 to October 9, 1982, the artist has his first solo exhibition at Galerie Bruno Bischofberger in Zurich: *Jean-Michel Basquiat*. On show, among other works, are *Profit I, Man from Naples, Crown Hotel, Four Big*, and *Multiflavors* (all 1982), which Bischofberger had previously purchased in New York. Basquiat travels to Switzerland for the first time on the eve of the show's opening, together with his assistant Stephen Torton. In the next few days, Bischofberger shows him around rural Eastern Switzerland, including Bischofberger's native place, the canton of Appenzell.

During Bischofberger's next visit to New York, Basquiat presents him with *Bruno in Appenzell* (p. 17), which depicts his gallerist surrounded by mountains, fir trees, the word *"Essen"* (German for food, because they ate at many local restaurants), and the crossed-out phrase "Stoss versus Stoss," as Bischofberger had also taken the artist to the Stoss Pass in Gais, where, in 1405, the people of Appenzell emerged victorious in their first great battle of the wars against the Habsburgs.

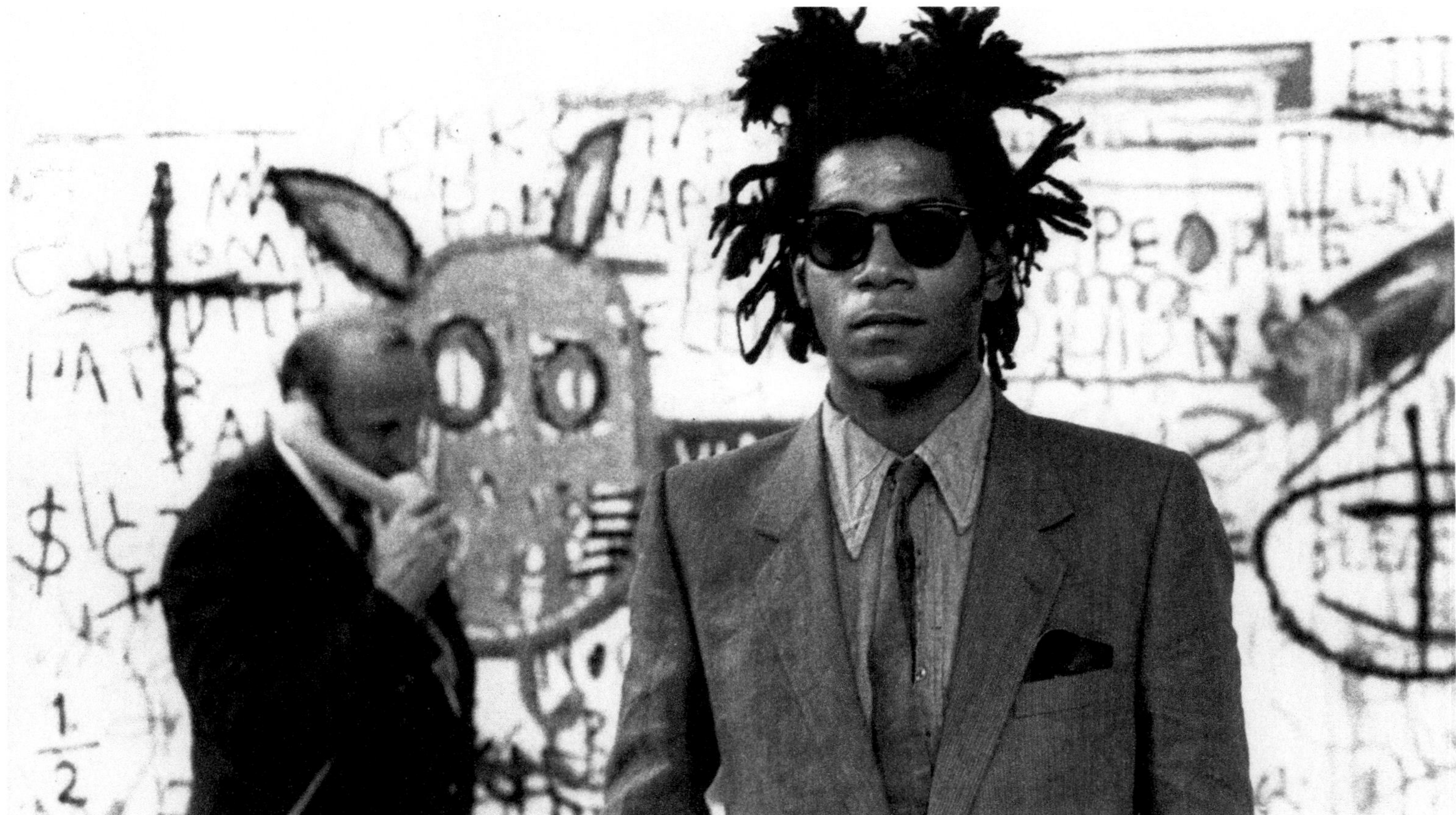

Jean-Michel Basquiat, with Bruno Bischofberger in the background, Galerie Bruno Bischofberger, Zurich, 1982

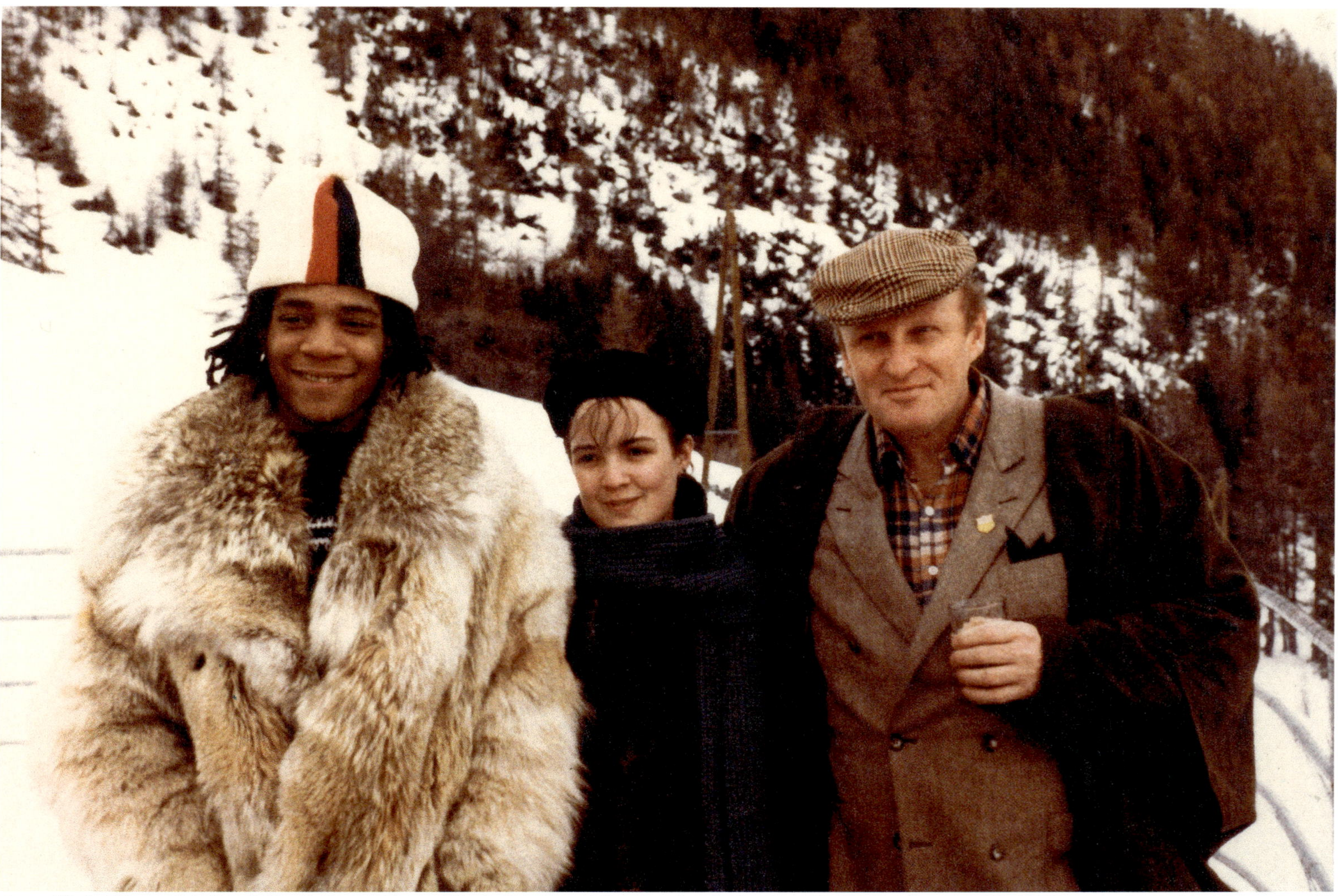

Jean-Michel Basquiat, Brook Bartlett, and Bruno Bischofberger at the Cresta clubhouse, St. Moritz, January 30, 1983

1983

January

Basquiat spends a few days with Bischofberger and his family at their house in St. Moritz, the Chesa Lodisa, where he will continue to visit once or twice every year, in winter or summer.

Together with Bischofberger and Brook Bartlett, an artist friend of Basquiat's in the early 1980s, Basquiat visits the clubhouse for the Cresta skeleton run in St. Moritz.

Famous Merchant and Seaman (p. 36) and the two paintings of Bischofberger's wife called *Yoyo (Portrait of Christina Bischofberger)* (pp. 38–39) are probably created during this stay.

May

Galerie Bruno Bischofberger loans pieces by Basquiat for the group exhibition *BACK TO THE USA: American Art of the 70s and 80s. Pattern & Decoration, New Image, New Wave, New Expressionism, Graffiti* (May 29–July 24, 1983) at the Kunstmuseum Luzern.

Summer

After traveling from Los Angeles to, among other places, Thailand and Tokyo (where Basquiat was invited to walk in an Issey Miyake fashion show), the artist concludes his trip by flying to Zurich. From there, he continues to Bischofberger's holiday home in St. Moritz, where Basquiat paints (in the garage, since no studio had yet been built) onto a brand-new custom-made mattress being stored there. Bischofberger buys the piece, called *Punch Bag* (p. 7), and—with Basquiat's permission—has the fabric removed from the mattress and stretched onto a frame.

During this stay, Bischofberger tells the artist that he has organized a dinner in his honor for the coming weekend, inviting guests interested in art, such as Stavros Niarchos, along with his sons Spyros and Philip, and Gianni and Marella Agnelli—both families live nearby in St. Moritz—as well as Johannes and Gloria von Thurn und Taxis. Basquiat has to go to New York for a day, but wants to come back for the dinner later that week. Since Bischofberger has no modern art hanging in the house that summer, only large-format photographs of the Engadin by Albert Steiner, Basquiat tells him he will paint some "hunting-lodge pictures" for the dinner. This motif goes well with the house's existing decor: antlers from a stag, a chamois, an Alpine ibex, and a roebuck, as well as a *Lusterweibchen* chandelier made from deer antlers. The dining room also has late Gothic and Baroque furniture decorated with ibexes and hunting motifs. In a short space of time, the five small works—*Skifahrer* (Skier; p. 25), *Nachtleben* (Nightlife; p. 26), *See* (Lake; p. 28), *Alpendorf* (Alpine Village; p. 29), and *Swiss House on Fire*—are created on the terrace of Chesa Lodisa.

On that same terrace, Basquiat creates *Swiss Son* (p. 22), which depicts Bischofberger with his son Magnus and a large "M" (for Magnus), framed by some of the carved Latin script from the ceiling of the (now closed) Pensiun Chasté inn in Sils Baselgia. At the bottom, the wood of Bischofberger's terrace appears in orange, along with trees from the surrounding area and parts of the ski lift next to the house.

September
At Basquiat's request, Bischofberger takes him, directly after his arrival at Zurich Airport, to Neu St. Johann in Toggenburg, St. Gallen, to attend a bull show in the district of Sidwald. Here, bulls are assessed, ranked, and the best ultimately crowned. That same day, fascinated by the atmosphere, the monumental bulls, and the traditional cuisine, Basquiat uses some paper he brought with him in a portfolio to create his four *Bull Show* drawings in a room at the Ochsen restaurant, where he was originally planning to recover from jet lag (pp. 31–35).
On a further trip to Appenzell Innerrhoden, Basquiat and Bischofberger hike to the alpine pastures of Alp Bommen below the Ebenalp, where they attend the preparations of dairy farmer Paul Peterer (a friend of Bischofberger's) for his cattle's descent from the pasture, as part of the Swiss tradition of *Alpabzug*. They then accompany the beautifully decorated cows via Weissbad to Appenzell and on to Unterschlatt. There, the farmer's family invites them to an early dinner with everybody who took part in the cattle drive.
From September 28 to October 22, 1983, Basquiat has his second solo exhibition at Zurich's Galerie Bruno Bischofberger: *Jean-Michel Basquiat: New Paintings.* Among other works, the exhibition presents *Hardware Store*, *Maurice*, *Toussaint L'Ouverture versus Savonarola*, and *Florence* (all 1983).
During a lunch at Restaurant Buech in Herrliberg, Zurich, where Bischofberger has regularly treated his friends and the gallery's artists over the years, Basquiat draws *Bratwurst* in the restaurant's guest book.

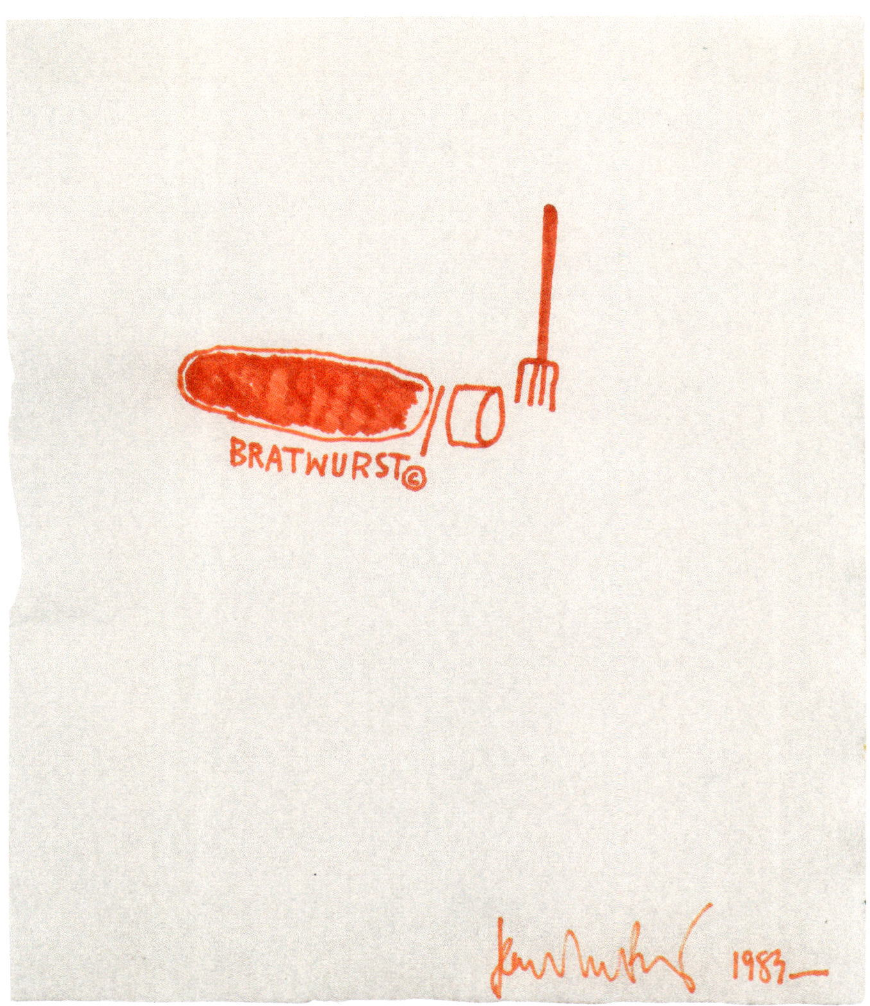

Bratwurst, 1983, 26.3 × 23.1 cm. From the guestbook of the Restaurant Buech, Herrliberg, Zurich

October
Basquiat takes part in the group show *Expressive Painting after Picasso* at Galerie Beyeler, Basel, where he shows *The Philistines* (1982), *Self-Portrait* (1982), *Stroll* (1982), and *BAP* (1983). The exhibition also includes works by Pablo Picasso, Joan Miró, Jean Dubuffet, Willem de Kooning, and Francis Bacon. *The Philistines* is selected for the cover of the exhibition catalogue.

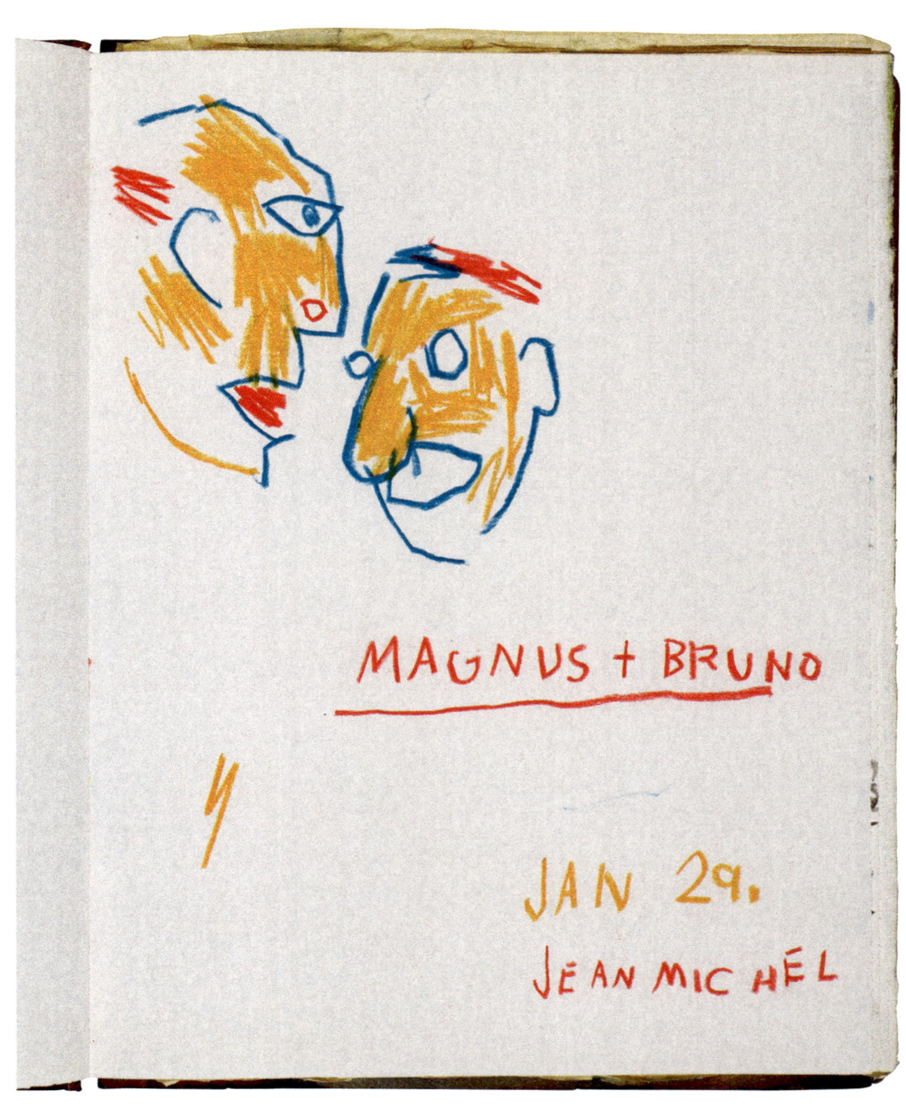

Magnus + Bruno, 1983, 30 × 23.7 cm. From the guestbook of Chesa Lodisa, St. Moritz, no. 1

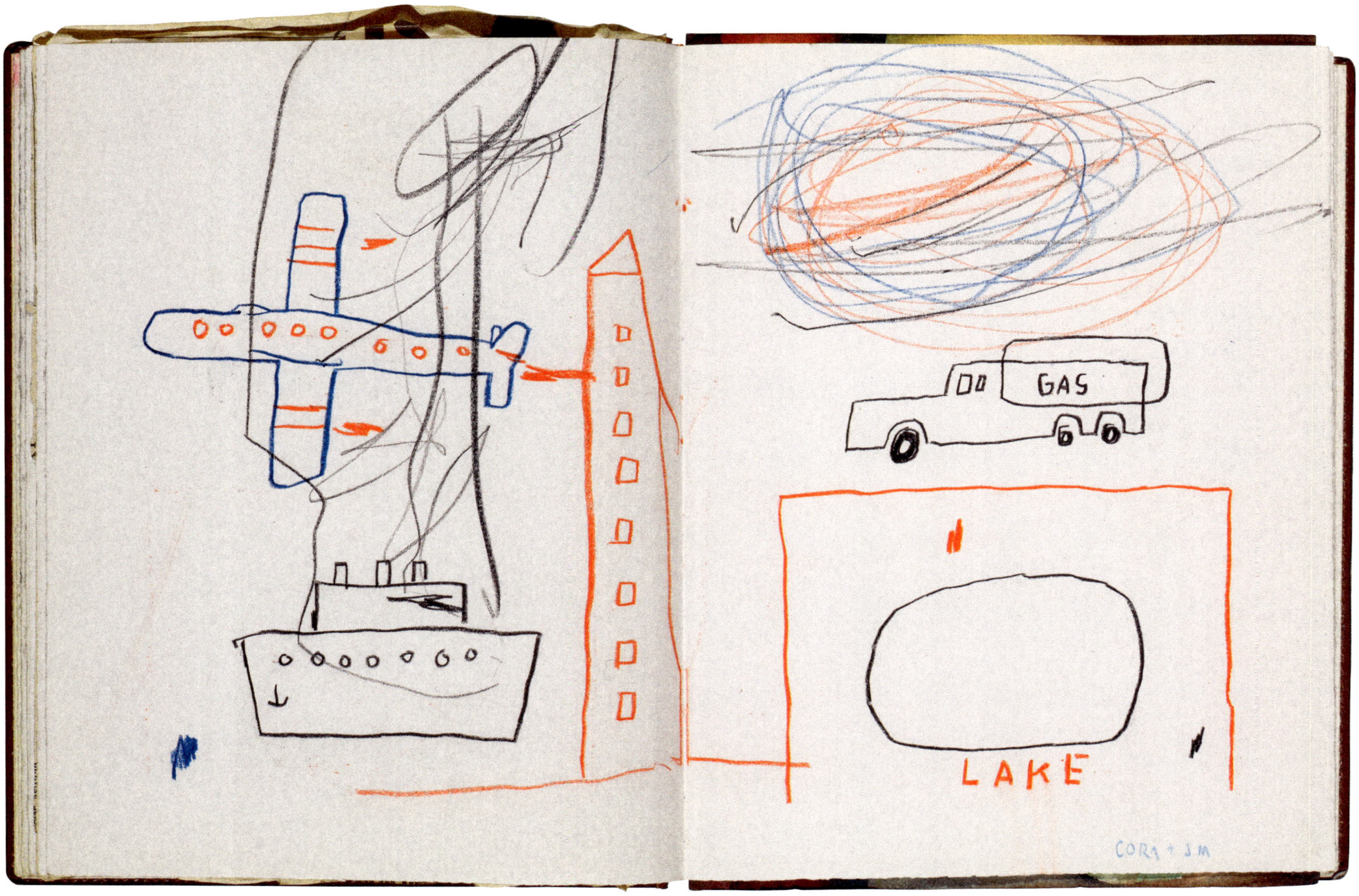

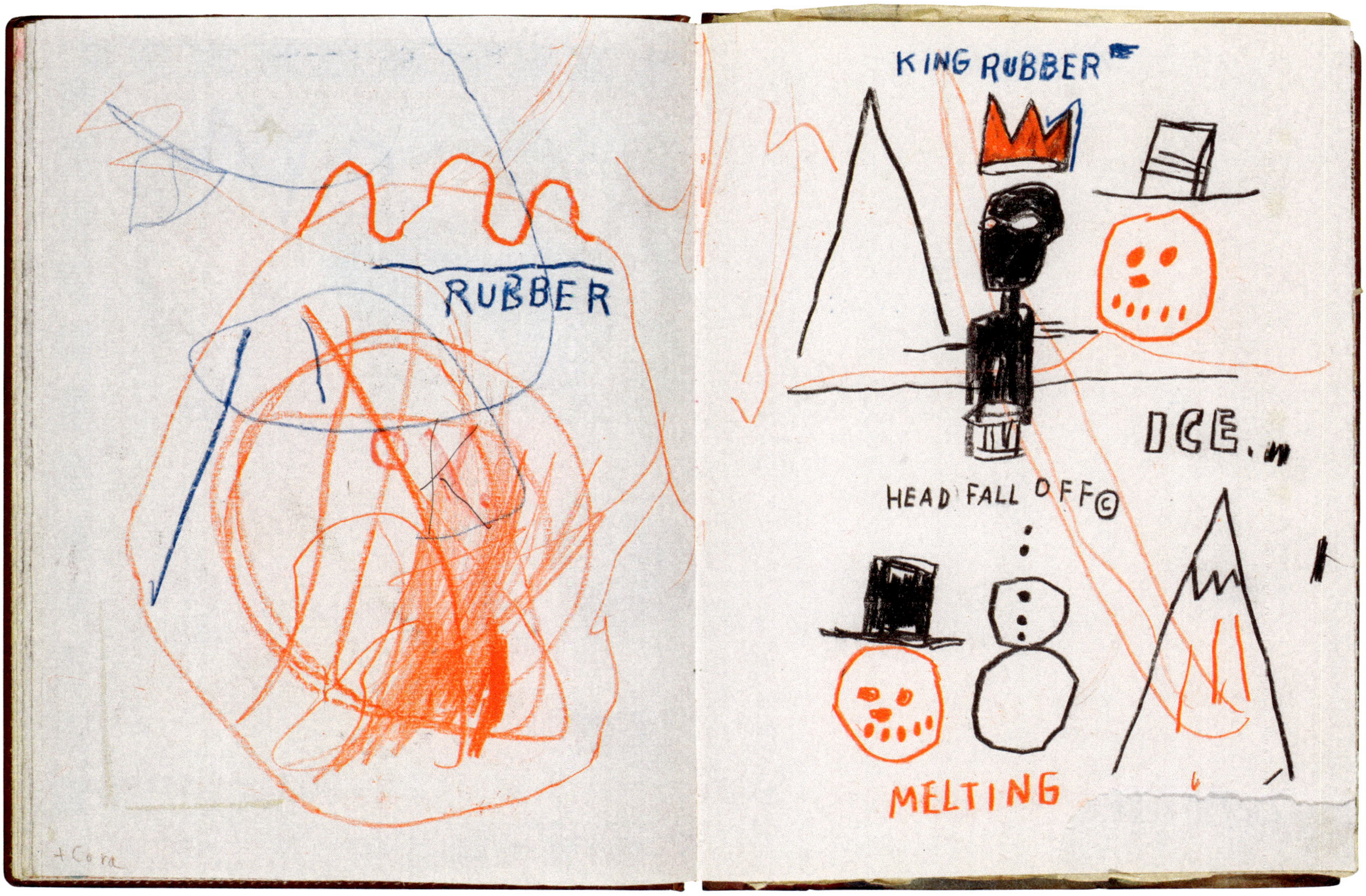

Top and bottom: Jean-Michel Basquiat and Cora Bischofberger, Untitled, 1984, 30 × 47.4 cm.
From the guestbook of Chesa Lodisa, St. Moritz, no. 1

1984

Winter
During another of Basquiat's visits to St. Moritz, Bischofberger
develops the idea for a groundbreaking collaboration between
Jean-Michel Basquiat, Andy Warhol, and Francesco Clemente.
Catalysts for this include Basquiat's collaborative work with
Cora, Bischofberger's then four-year-old daughter, among these
the painting Untitled (Pakiderm) (1983; p. 44) and the two
Untitled (Guestbook Chesa Lodisa no. 1; 1984, p.69) drawings
in the family guest book.

Summer
Basquiat travels with the Bischofbergers (both parents and all
four children) in a rented private jet from St. Moritz to Italy.
In Ancona they see the artist Enzo Cucchi, and in Rome they
visit Francesco Clemente to have a family portrait made.
During a break, Basquiat, Clemente, and Bischofberger go
to the nearby restaurant Casa del Popolo. There, the two
artists discuss and title the fifteen works Basquiat, Clemente,
and Warhol have meanwhile created together in New York.
The name of the restaurant becomes the title of one. From Rome,
they travel on to the Spanish island of Majorca to visit the
artist Miquel Barceló. Afterward, they return to St. Moritz, where
Basquiat paints the large-format family portrait *The Bischofbergers* (p. 13) in the gravel patio beside the family's house.

September
From September 15 to October 13, 1984, Galerie Bruno Bischofberger in Zurich shows the fifteen commissioned collaborative works under the title *Collaborations: Basquiat Clemente
Warhol*. A publication of the same name accompanies the
exhibition.

Christmas
Basquiat spends Christmas with the Bischofbergers at their
St. Moritz home. As a Christmas gift for each family member,
he presents one of the eighteen paintings with crowned, mask-
like heads that he created in the studio of the Norwegian
artist Knut Swane in Stockholm and sent by post to St. Moritz
(p. 48).

1985

January
From January 19 to February 16, 1985, Basquiat has his third
solo exhibition at Galerie Bruno Bischofberger. *Jean-Michel
Basquiat: New Works* brings together eleven new pieces,
including *P-Z*, *Zydeco*, *Max Roach*, and *M* (all 1984).

June
From June 20 to October 20, 1985, Basquiat takes part in the
group exhibition *The Engadine in Painting* at the Segantini
Museum in St. Moritz. The exhibition features the painting *See*,
depicting an Engadin lake, which is one of the artist's few
landscape representations (see Summer 1983).

July–August
During a stay with the Bischofbergers, Basquiat spontaneously
decides to take a taxi to Italy with a young friend interning
at the Palace Hotel St. Moritz and visits Portofino, Carrara,
and Florence.
Bischofberger wants to support Basquiat's wish
of exhibiting his work in one of the countries of his African
ancestors, although the artist doesn't know exactly where they
came from. During another of the artist's stays in the Engadin,
Bischofberger takes him to S-chanf, where he introduces him
to his friend Claudio Caratsch, who is the Swiss ambassador
to Ivory Coast during this time. With Caratsch's help, the gallerist
organizes an exhibition at the Centre Culturel Français in
the capital city of Abidjan, to be held the next year. Caratsch
explains to Basquiat that, in many parts of Africa, art is not
made exclusively for art's sake, as it is in the West, but to enact
a specific purpose, such as "to repel ghosts." Amused that
the ambassador is telling him something he already knows,
Basquiat says nothing. In St. Moritz, he then creates two
smaller works called *To Repel Ghosts* (pp. 55–56), on which he
inscribes that phrase. In 1986, Basquiat produces another
piece by that name on a wooden piece broken during the
new construction being done at Bischofberger's gallery in
Zurich (p. 53).

1986

April
Jean-Michel Basquiat: Drawings is on show from April 26
to June 30, 1986, at Galerie Bruno Bischofberger. It is his
fourth solo exhibition at the gallery and presents a selection
of twenty-five drawings from 1984 to 1986.

October
With the help of Caratsch, Bischofberger organizes an
exhibition at the Centre Culturel Français in Abidjan
from October 10 to November 7, 1986. Basquiat travels to
Ivory Coast with his girlfriend Jennifer Goode and her
brother Eric and meets Yoyo and Bruno Bischofberger there.
Together, they travel onward to Korhogo in the north,
where they meet with the Senufo people.

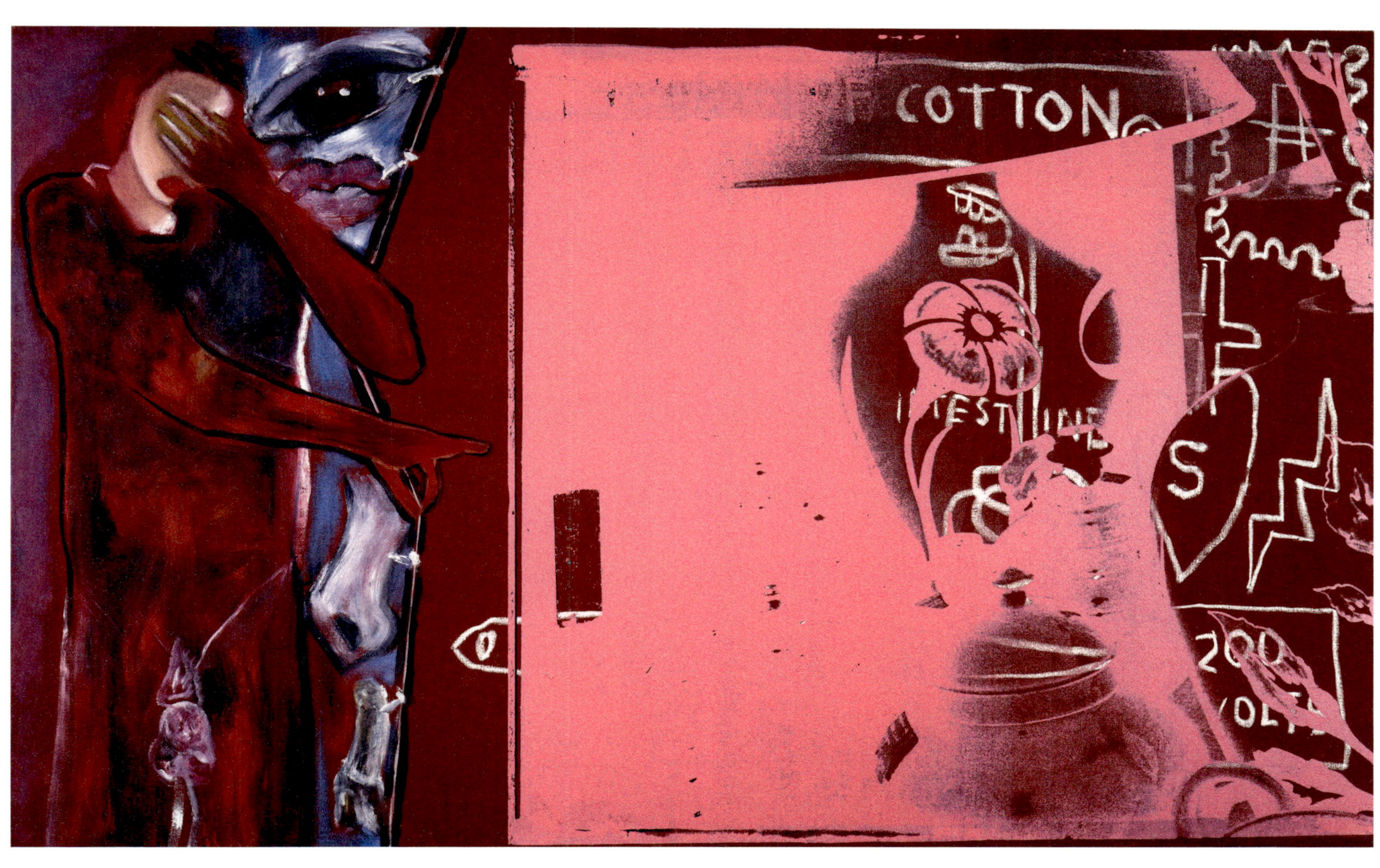

Jean-Michel Basquiat, Francesco Clemente, and Andy Warhol, *Casa del Popolo*, 1984, 128 × 215 cm

November
The exhibition *Collaborations: Jean-Michel Basquiat and Andy Warhol* (November 14, 1986–January 17, 1987) opens at Galerie Bruno Bischofberger, showing around ten new collaborative works made between late 1984 and mid-1985.

Compiled by Sophie Wratzfeld together with Bruno Bischofberger and Silvia Sokalski

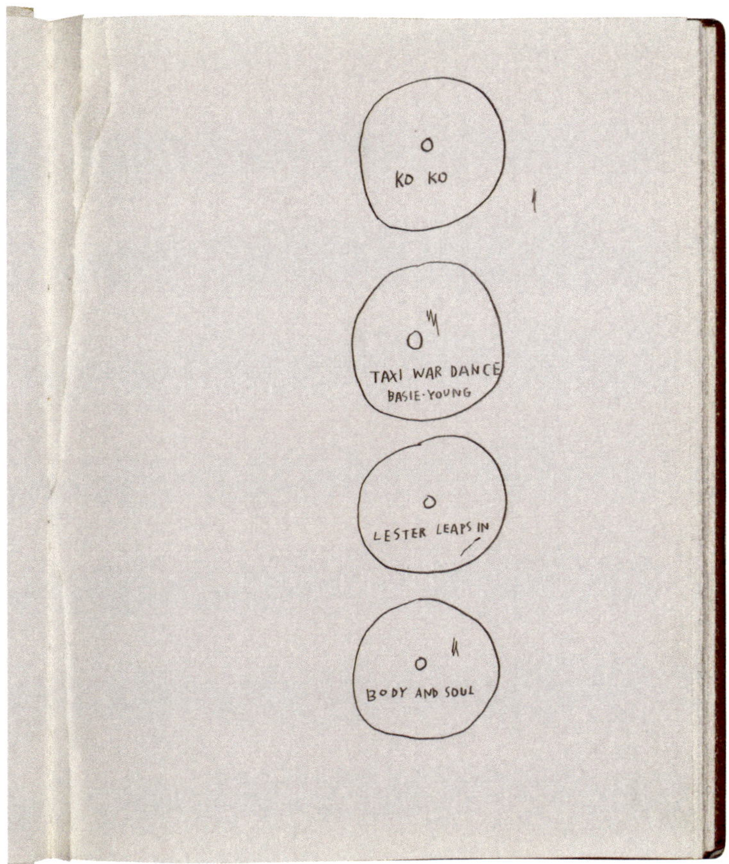

Untitled (Four Records), 1986, 30 × 23.7 cm. From the guestbook of Chesa Lodisa, St. Moritz, no. 1

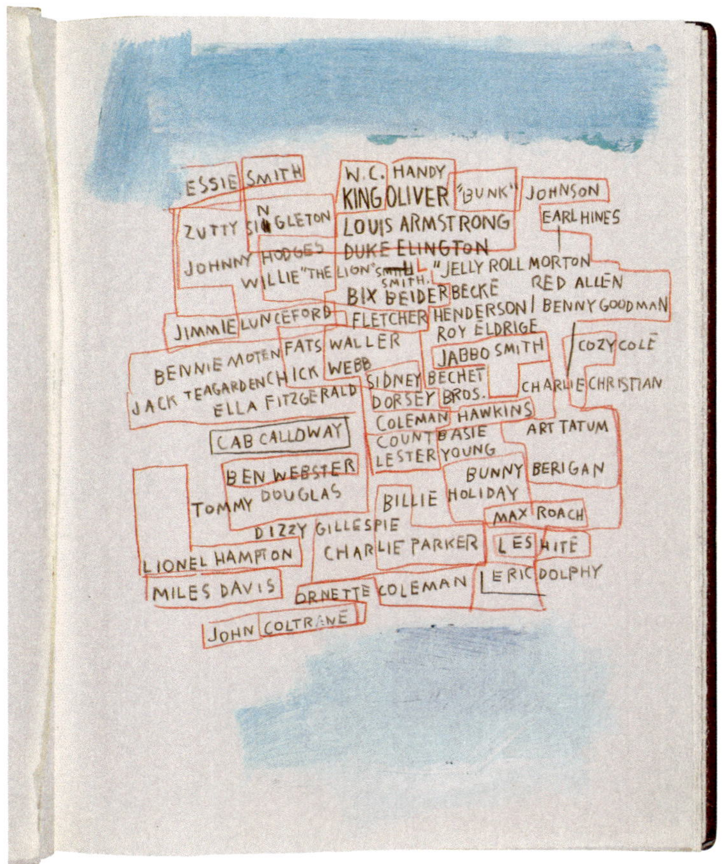

Untitled (Jazz Musicians), 1986, 30 × 23.7 cm. From the guestbook of Chesa Lodisa, St. Moritz, no. 1

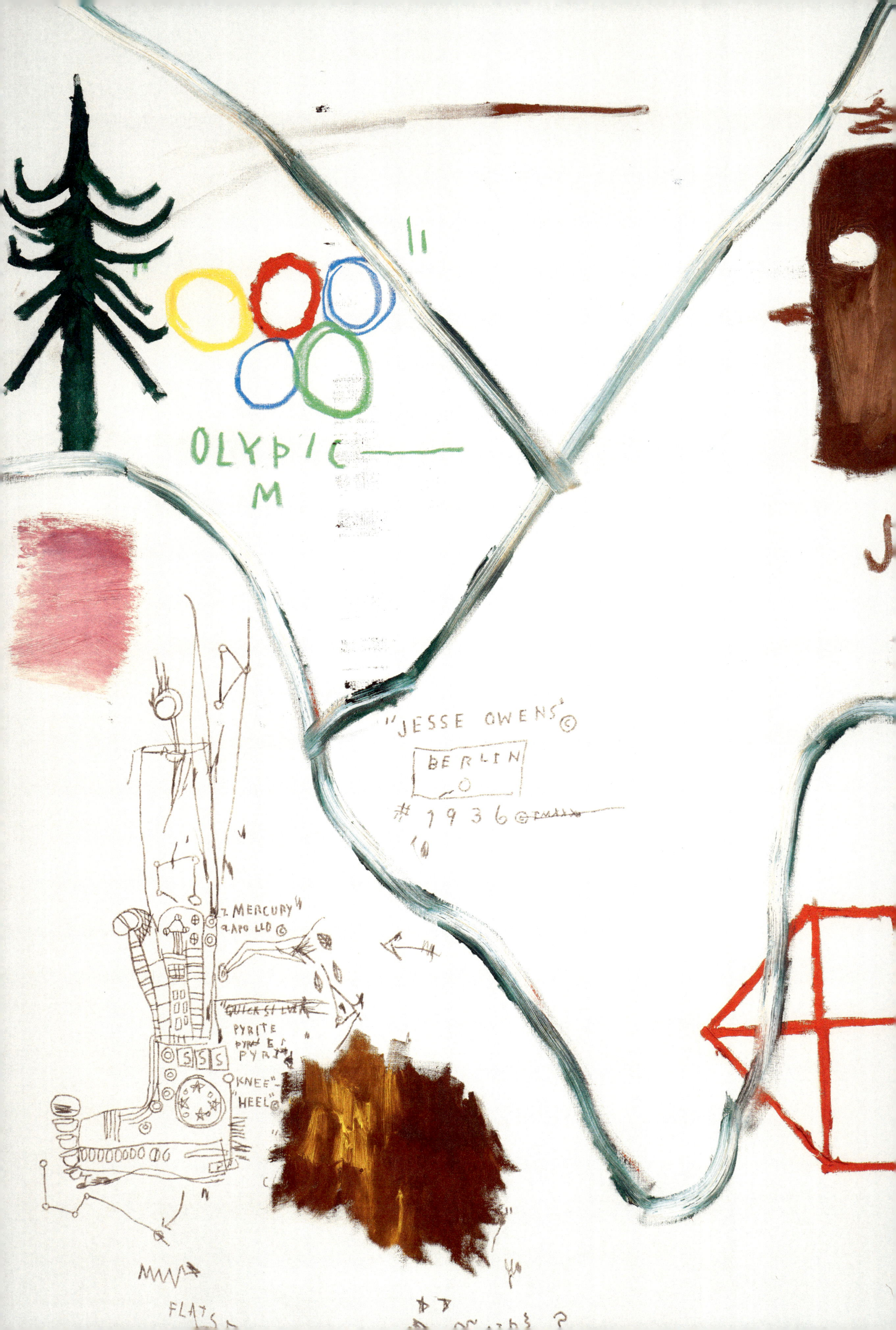

OLYMPIC
M
"JESSE OWENS"©
BERLIN
1936
z. MERCURY
R.APOLLO ©
QUICKSILVER
PYRITE
PYRITES
PYRITE
"KNEE"
"HEEL"
SSS
FLATS

List of Illustrated Works

Punch Bag, 1983
Acrylic and oil stick on linen
187 × 157 cm (73 ⅝ × 61 ¾ in.)
p. 7

The Bischofbergers, 1984
Acrylic on canvas
162 × 202 cm (63 ¾ × 79 ½ in.)
Bischofberger Collection, Männedorf-Zurich
p. 13 *

Bruno in Appenzell, 1982
Acrylic and oil on canvas
140 × 140 cm (55 ⅛ × 55 ⅛ in.)
Bischofberger Collection, Männedorf-Zurich
p. 17 *

The Dutch Settlers, 1982
Acrylic and oil stick on canvas
183 × 549 cm (72 × 216 ⅛ in.)
Nicola Erni Collection
pp. 20–21 *

Swiss Son, 1983
Acrylic on canvas
160 × 200 cm (63 × 78 ¾ in.)
Bischofberger Collection, Männedorf-Zurich
p. 22; p. 8 (detail) *

Skifahrer (Skier), 1983
Oil on canvas
70 × 90 cm (27 ½ × 35 ⅜ in.)
Collection Carmignac
p. 25 *

Nachtleben (Nightlife), 1983
Acrylic and oil stick on canvas
100 × 100 cm (39 ⅜ × 39 ⅜ in.)
Heidi Horten Collection, Vienna
p. 26

See (Lake), 1983
Oil on canvas
101 × 101 cm (39 ¾ × 39 ¾ in.)
Private collection
p. 28 *

Alpendorf (Alpine Village), 1983
Acrylic on canvas
102 × 102 cm (40 ⅛ × 40 ⅛ in.)
Heidi Horten Collection, Vienna
p. 29

Bull Show One, 1983
Mixed media on paper
51 × 73 cm (20 ⅛ × 28 ¾ in.)
Bischofberger Collection, Männedorf-Zurich
p. 31; p. 32 (detail) *

Bull Show Two, 1983
Mixed media on paper
51 × 73 cm (20 ⅛ × 28 ¾ in.)
Bischofberger Collection, Männedorf-Zurich
p. 33 *

Bull Show Three, 1983
Mixed media on paper
51 × 73 cm (20 ⅛ × 28 ¾ in.)
Bischofberger Collection, Männedorf-Zurich
p. 34; p. 4 (detail) *

Bull Show Four, 1983
Mixed media on paper
51 × 73 cm (20 ⅛ × 28 ¾ in.)
Bischofberger Collection, Männedorf-Zurich
p. 35 *

Famous Merchant and Seaman, 1983
Oil and oil stick on canvas
70 × 50 cm (27 ½ × 19 ¾ in.)
Bischofberger Collection, Männedorf-Zurich
p. 36 *

Yoyo (Portrait of Christina Bischofberger), 1983
Mixed media on canvas
70.5 × 50 cm (27 ¾ × 19 ¾ in.)
Bischofberger Collection, Männedorf-Zurich
p. 38 *

Yoyo (Portrait of Christina Bischofberger), 1983
Mixed media on canvas
70.5 × 50 cm (27 ¾ × 19 ¾ in.)
Bischofberger Collection, Männedorf-Zurich
p. 39 *

Bratwurst (Portrait of Bruno Bischofberger), 1983
Mixed media on paper
29.2 × 41.5 cm (11 ½ × 16 ⅜ in.)
Bischofberger Collection, Männedorf-Zurich
p. 42 (top) *

Showbull, 1983
Mixed media on paper
41.5 × 29.2 cm (16 ⅜ × 11 ½ in.)
Bischofberger Collection, Männedorf-Zurich
p. 42 (left) *

Eingang (Entrance), 1983
Mixed media on paper
41.5 × 29.2 cm (16 ⅜ × 11 ½ in.)
Bischofberger Collection, Männedorf-Zurich
p. 42 (right) *

Bratwurst, 1983
Oil stick and charcoal on paper
41.5 × 29.2 cm (16 ⅜ × 11 ½ in.)
Bischofberger Collection, Männedorf-Zurich
p. 43 (top) *

Appenzeller Alpenbitter ©, 1983
Charcoal on paper
70 × 100 cm (27 ½ × 39 ⅜ in.)
Bischofberger Collection, Männedorf-Zurich
p. 43 (bottom) *

Jean-Michel Basquiat and Cora Bischofberger
Untitled (Pakiderm), 1983
Acrylic and oil stick on canvas
120 × 120 cm (47 ¼ × 47 ¼ in.)
Cora Sheibani-Bischofberger Collection
p. 44; p. 64 (detail) *

Jean-Michel Basquiat, Francesco Clemente,
and Andy Warhol
In Bianco (In White), 1984
Acrylic, silk screen, and pastel on canvas
122 × 168 cm (48 × 66 ⅛ in.)
Fundación Almine y Bernard Ruiz-Picasso,
Madrid
p. 47 *

X-mas Painting for Bruno, 1984
Mixed media on canvas
81 × 81 cm (31 ⅞ × 31 ⅞ in.)
Bischofberger Collection, Männedorf-Zurich
p. 48; p. 14 (detail) *

Big Snow, 1984
Acrylic and oil stick on canvas
168 × 151.5 cm (66 ⅛ × 59 ⅝ in.)
Private collection
p. 50; p. 74 (detail) *

To Repel Ghosts, 1986
Acrylic on wood
112 × 83 × 10 cm (44 ⅛ × 32 ⅝ × 4 in.)
Nicola Erni Collection
p. 53 *

To Repel Ghosts, 1986
Oil on canvas
35.6 × 41.2 cm (14 × 16 ¼ in.)
George Condo Collection, New York
(acquired 1986)
p. 55 *

To Repel Ghosts, 1986
Oil on canvas
30.5 × 50.2 cm (12 × 19 ¾ in.)
George Condo Collection, New York
(acquired 1986)
p. 56 *

Worthy Constituents, 1986
Acrylic, collage, oil stick, pencil, and coffee
on canvas
70 × 90 cm (27 ½ × 35 ⅜ in.)
Bischofberger Collection, Männedorf-Zurich
p. 59 *

Self-Portrait, 1984
Acrylic and oil stick on paper mounted on
canvas
100 × 70 cm (39 ⅜ × 27 ½ in.)
Collection Yoav Harlap, courtesy Safdie Fine Art
Ltd
p. 62; p. 1 (detail)

Bratwurst, 1983
From the guestbook of the Restaurant Buech,
Herrliberg, Zurich
Felt pen on paper
26.3 × 23.1 cm (10 ⅜ × 9 ⅛ in.)
Bischofberger Collection, Männedorf-Zurich
p. 67

Magnus + Bruno, 1983
From the guestbook of Chesa Lodisa, St. Moritz,
no. 1
Mixed media on paper
30 × 23.7 cm (11 ¾ × 9 ⅜ in.)
Bischofberger Collection, Männedorf-Zurich
p. 68

Jean-Michel Basquiat and Cora Bischofberger
Untitled, 1984
From the guestbook of Chesa Lodisa, St. Moritz,
no. 1
30 × 47.4 cm (11 ¾ × 18 ⅝ in.)
Bischofberger Collection, Männedorf-Zurich
p. 69 (top)

Jean-Michel Basquiat and Cora Bischofberger
Untitled, 1984
From the guestbook of Chesa Lodisa, St. Moritz,
no. 1
30 × 47.4 cm (11 ¾ × 18 ⅝ in.)
Bischofberger Collection, Männedorf-Zurich
p. 69 (bottom)

Jean-Michel Basquiat, Francesco Clemente,
and Andy Warhol
Casa del Popolo, 1984
Mixed media on canvas
128 × 215 cm (50 ⅜ × 84 ⅝ in.)
Private collection
p. 71

Untitled (Four Records), 1986
From the guestbook of Chesa Lodisa, St. Moritz,
no. 1
Mixed media on paper
30 × 23.7 cm (11 ¾ × 9 ⅜ in.)
Bischofberger Collection, Männedorf-Zurich
p. 72 (left)

Untitled (Jazz Musicians), 1986
From the guestbook of Chesa Lodisa, St. Moritz,
no. 1
Mixed media on paper
30 × 23.7 cm (11 ¾ × 9 ⅜ in.)
Bischofberger Collection, Männedorf-Zurich
p. 72 (right)

* included in the exhibition

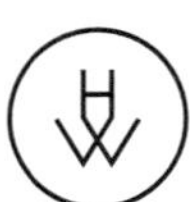

Publisher: Michaela Unterdörfer
Managing editor: Maria Elena Garzoni
Editorial support: Anna Karina Hofbauer,
Sophie Wratzfeld (Buchhart Hofbauer);
Silvia Sokalski (Galerie Bruno Bischofberger)
Copyediting: Jaclyn Arndt
Proofreading: Julia Monks
Translation: Brian Currid, Florian Duijens

Book design and typography: Christian Knöpfel
Production coordination: Christine Stäcker
Prepress: LUP, Cologne
Printing: Offsetdruckerei Karl Grammlich,
Pliezhausen, Germany
Binding: Josef Spinner Großbuchbinderei GmbH,
Ottersweier, Germany

Cover Paper: Wibalin Natural white, 120 gsm
Endpapers: Wibalin Recycled basalt, 120 gsm
Paper: Profibulk 1.3 Vol, 135 gsm
Typeface: ABC Pelikan, Basel Grotesk

Jean-Michel Basquiat: Engadin
© 2025 Hauser & Wirth Publishers
www.hauserwirth.com

Distribution:
North and South America
ARTBOOK | D.A.P.
75 Broad Street, Suite 630
New York, NY 10004
artbook.com

Germany
Buchhandlung Walther König
Ehrenstrasse 4
50672 Cologne
buchhandlung-walther-koenig.de

All other territories
Thames & Hudson Ltd.
181A High Holborn
London WC1V 7QX
thamesandhudson.com

ISBN: 978-3-907493-02-1
Library of Congress Control Number:
2024949544

Printed and bound in Germany

Published on the occasion of the exhibition
Jean-Michel Basquiat: Engadin
Hauser & Wirth, Via Serlas 22, St. Moritz
(Switzerland)
December 14, 2024 – March 29, 2025

Exhibition team: Dr. Dr. Dieter Buchhart,
Dr. Anna Karina Hofbauer, Sophie Wratzfeld, MA;
Giorgia von Albertini, Nicole Keller, James Koch

The exhibition would not have been possible
without the generosity of the lenders. Our
gratitude goes to the Bischofberger Collection,
Männedorf-Zurich; Collection Carmignac;
George Condo Collection, New York; Nicola
Erni Collection; Fundación Almine y Bernard
Ruiz-Picasso, Madrid; Cora Sheibani-
Bischofberger Collection; and others who
prefer to remain anonymous.
        We would also like to thank Nora
Fitzpatrick, Lisane Basquiat, and Jeanine
Heriveaux from the Estate of Jean-Michel
Basquiat; David Stark and Sara Citarella from
Artestar; and Silvia Sokalski, Nicole Kaltenbach,
Sven Gehrke, Gary Kammerhuber, and Martina
Schwaninger from Galerie Bruno Bischofberger
for their support of this ambitious project.